Old Testament Poetry & Prophecy

James L. R. Catron

EMMAUS
WORLDWIDE

Developed as a study course by Emmaus Correspondence School, founded in 1942.

Old Testament Poetry & Prophecy
James L. R. Catron

Published by:
Emmaus Worldwide
PO Box 1028
Dubuque, IA 52004-1028
phone: (563) 585-2070
email: info@EmmausWorldwide.com
website: EmmausWorldwide.com

First Edition 1993 (AK '93), 2 UNITS
Revised 2005 (AK '05), 2 UNITS
Reprinted 2008 (AK '05), 2 UNITS
Reprinted 2012 (AK '05), 2 UNITS
Reprinted 2018 (AK '18), 2 UNITS
Revised 2020 (AK '20), 2 UNITS

ISBN 978-1-59387-501-5

Code: OTPP

Printed in the United States of America

Course Overview

Suffering, loneliness, anger, sorrow, and stress touch all of our lives. They are part of the human experience and always have been, even in the ancient world. The Poetry and Prophecy books of the Bible show us that these feelings are not unfamiliar even to biblical authors. These books can encourage us through the highs and lows of life, as well as call us to repentance when we stray from God. This survey course is designed to introduce you to two types of biblical literature, Poetry and Prophecy, and their place in biblical history, with relevant application to God's people today.

Lessons You Will Study

Student Instructions

This Emmaus course is designed to help you know God through a better understanding of the Bible and know how it applies to your life. However, this course can never take the place of the Bible itself. The Bible is inexhaustible, and no course could give the full meaning of its truth. If studying this course is the end goal, it will become an obstacle to your growth; if it is used to inspire and equip you for your own personal study of the Bible, then it will achieve its goal. As you study the Bible using this course, prayerfully ask God to reveal His truth to you in a powerful way.

Course Sections

This course has three parts: the *lessons*, the *exams* and the *exam sheet*.

The Lessons

Each lesson is written to help explain truths from the Bible. Read each lesson through at least twice—once to get a general idea of its content, then again, slowly, looking up any Bible references given. You should always have your Bible opened to the verses or passage being studied. It is important that you read the Bible passages referenced, as some questions in the exams may be based on the Bible text.

To look up a Bible verse, keep in mind passages in the Bible are listed by book, chapter, and verse. For instance, 2 Peter 1:21 refers to the second book of Peter, chapter 1, and verse 21. At the beginning of every Bible, there is a table of contents which lists the names of the books of the Bible and tells the page number on which each book begins. For practice, look up 2 Peter in the table of contents and turn to the page number listed; then find the chapter and verse.

The Exams

At the end of each lesson, there is an exam to assess your knowledge of the course material and the Bible passages. The exams contain multiple choice and/or True/False (T/F) questions. After you have studied a lesson, complete the exam for that lesson by recording your answers on the exam sheet that has been provided. If you have difficulty answering the questions, re-read the lesson or use the Bible as a reference.

Please note, it is best not to answer the questions based on what you *think* or have *always believed*. The questions are designed to find out if you understand the material in the course and the Bible.

What Do You Say?

In addition to the multiple choice section, each exam also contains a *What Do You Say?* question. These questions are designed for your personal reflection and to help you express your ideas and feelings as you process the lesson's content.

The Exam Sheet

Use the exam sheet provided by your group leader or instructor. When you have determined the right answer to a question on an exam, fill in the corresponding letter on the exam sheet. If you do not have someone who could provide an exam sheet, you can download one at www.emmausworldwide.org/exam-sheets

Submitting the Exam Sheet

When you have answered all the exam questions on the exam sheet, check them carefully. Fill in your contact information and submit your completed exam sheet to your group leader or instructor or the organization from which you received it (several options for submission are shown at next page).

OPTION 1: Send to your group leader or instructor

If you know your group leader or instructor, give them your completed exam sheet or mail it to the address listed here (if blank, go to option 2).

OPTION 2: Send to Emmaus Worldwide's head office

If no address is listed above, or if you do not know if you have a group leader or instructor and are unsure of where to send your exam sheet, choose one of the following:

MAIL the exam sheet to

Emmaus Worldwide
PO Box 1028
Dubuque, IA 52004-1028

OR

EMAIL a scan or photo

of both sides of the exam sheet to this email address:

Exams@EmmauWorldwide.org

Receiving Your Results

You will receive back your graded exam sheet (through the same method it was submitted, either mail or email), including your final grade and a personal response from your group leader or instructor or Emmaus Worldwide.

Introduction to the Poetic Books, and Job

The Old Testament is made up of thirty-nine books. These are divided into the categories of *Law* (Genesis–Deuteronomy), *History* (Joshua–Esther), *Poetry* (Job–Song of Solomon), and *Prophecy* (Isaiah–Malachi). This course is devoted to a survey of the poetic and prophetic books. A *survey* is simply an overview. It does not present each book in detail. It helps the reader to know generally what is in each book, how the book flows, who wrote the book, and when it was written. One value of a survey is that it prepares us to study a book more intelligently in detail later on. Another value is that it helps us to see the Bible as a unified whole. The survey, then, is basic to any diligent study and detailed understanding of God's holy Word.

Time Location of the Poetic Books

Though one will find poetry here and there in the law and historic books and much poetry in the prophetic books, there are five books which are especially labeled as books of poetry: Job, Psalms, Proverbs, Ecclesiastes, and Song of Solomon.

The setting of Job was during the time of the Old Testament patriarchs covered in Genesis 12–50. Many believe that Moses wrote it. The Psalms were primarily written during the era of David, though some og them were written as early as Moses' time and others as late as Ezra's day. Solomon, whose history is given in 1 Kings 1–11 and 2 Chronicles 1–9, wrote Proverbs, Ecclesiastes, and Song of Solomon.

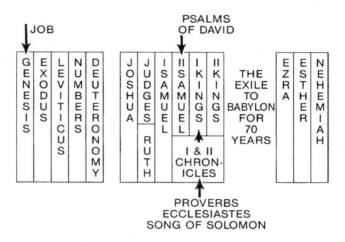

Themes of the Poetic Books

Job tells us how to suffer in the will of God (Job 1:20-22; 2:10). The book of Psalms teaches us the art of prayer and praise to our God (Ps. 3 and 150). Proverbs instructs us how to live wisely on earth in the fear of God (Prov. 1:7). Ecclesiastes teaches us how to have true meaning and joy in life in fear of God (Eccl. 2:24-26; 12:13-14). Song of Solomon tells us how to have genuine love in courtship and marriage as God originally intended it (Song 8:6-7).

The Practical Character of the Poetic Books

The poetic books address many life situations which we face every day. Some of these are: suffering, fear, loneliness, anxiety, anger, hatred, sorrow, stress, disobedient children, confusion, and opposition. These books give sound advice on how to cope with these and a host of other problems.

Hebrew Poetry Found in the Poetic Books

In Western poetry, we are used to rhyme, but poetry in the Bible is not characterized by rhyme. Instead, Hebrew poetry uses *thought parallelism*. After the writer makes a statement in the first line of a verse, it is repeated, enlarged, or balanced by statements in the remaining line or lines. Let us note some examples of this.

Synonymous Parallelism (same idea, different words)

The second line repeats the thought of the first line.

> "Your steadfast love, O LORD, extends to the heavens,
> Your faithfulness to the clouds." Psalm 36:5

Antithetic Parallelism (opposite idea)

The idea of second line contrasts with the first line.

> "For the LORD knows the way of the righteous,
> But the way of the wicked will perish." Psalm 1:6

Synthetic Parallelism (several ideas drawn together to complete the idea)

The second and later lines explain or add something. There are three types of this parallelism:

Completion Type (Ps. 29:1)

We will see how "glory and strength" complete the thought.

> "Ascribe to the LORD, O heavenly beings,
> Ascribe to the LORD glory and strength."

Comparison Type (Prov. 15:17)

Often this type will use the words better … than.

> "Better is a dinner of herbs where love is
> Than a fattened ox and hatred with it."

Reason Type (Prov. 26:4)

> "Answer not a fool according to his folly,
> Lest you be like him yourself."

Emblematic Parallelism (Prov. 25:25) (Uses like … so is)

The first line serves as an emblem or illustration of the second line. "*Like* cold water to a thirsty soul, *so is* good news from a far country." Knowing something about parallelism makes it much easier to read through the poetic books and helps us properly interpret the poetic Scripture.

Because the poetic books are so practical in nature and universal in their appeal, you should read them often. It is unfortunate that these books are so neglected simply because they are written in poetic style. But don't stop with just reading them—memorize them as well. For instance many of the shorter psalms which deal with trust and praise are ideal to hide in your heart through memorization. Then they can become a constant source of strength and encouragement.

JOB

How to Suffer in the Will of God

Few people choose to suffer. We take great measures to protect ourselves and avoid suffering. Self-preservation is instinctive in man, yet suffering is a fact of life. Suffering began when our first parents sinned (Gen. 3) and it will remain until we are in heaven (Rev. 21:4).

The problem of pain is one that philosophers, theologians, and the average person have wrestled with from the very beginning. The book of Job is the outstanding book of the Bible that deals with personal suffering.

> **It is more important that we learn how to suffer than to know the reason behind suffering.**

Job is a long book with forty-two chapters and primarily concerns itself with the calamities that afflicted God's servant, Job. Job was not told why he had to suffer. The why of suffering was something he did not understand. God withheld from Job vital information (1:6-12; 2:1-8) which might have defeated God's purposes in this suffering if Job had known it.

We will learn from the book of Job that it is more important that we learn *how* to suffer than to know the reason behind suffering. Faith and submission are the two basic requirements for "successful" suffering in the will of God. Job brilliantly exercised both faith and submission in the beginning of his suffering (1:20-22; 2:9-10) but became distracted in the process of dealing with his grief (chapters 3-31). He later resumed these attitudes (chapters 38-42), and the story ended on a very bright and positive note (42:7-17).

It is easier to have faith and submit to God when we know the character of God. He is wise, just, and full of compassion. He has our best interests at heart and will never let us be tested beyond what we can bear (1 Cor. 10:13). We can trust Him (Ps. 55:22).

When Did the Story of Job Take Place?

Scholars have debated when Job lived, and probably the best answer is during the period of the patriarchs (Gen. 12–50). So many things in the book of Job resemble the history and culture during the time of Abraham, Isaac, and Jacob. However, not knowing the exact answer to this question does not prevent us from understanding the message of the book.

Who wrote the Book of Job?

Bible scholars do not agree totally about who wrote Job. Some believe Moses wrote it during his stay in Midian (1485–1445 BC, Exodus 2–3) for the purpose of comforting the people of Israel who were suffering in Egypt. Others prefer the time of Solomon (971–931 BC, 1 Kings 1-11) when so many wisdom books were being produced. Still others think that it was written as late as the seventh century BC during the reign of King Manasseh (2 Kings 21). This writer thinks that the authorship of Moses has the least problems. However, not knowing the identity of the author does not affect the interpretation of the book.

Who Was Job? A Character of Fiction or a Historic Figure?

Though there are some who claim that Job was not a real person, there is ample evidence from both the Old and New Testaments to prove that he was. The prophet Ezekiel, for instance, considered Job a historical person (Ezek. 14:14, 20) by linking him with Noah and Daniel. James, in the New Testament, leaves no doubt that he believed Job was a real person by linking Job with the Old Testament prophets (James 5:10-11). If Job were simply a fictional character, the message of the book would be far less forceful and much less effective in comforting those who suffer. May Job's life story be a source of great comfort and encouragement to you!

Who Are the Characters in the book of Job?

Job

Job was an incredible person of high character whom God commended to Satan as the greatest moral and spiritual man on the earth (1:8). Like so many others in the Bible, Job is a model for us.

The Lord

The Lord allowed Job to be severely tested. Job lost his wealth, his family, and his health. But God praised him for his faithfulness in the end (42:7-17). God uses testing in our lives to build into us character and endurance (James 5:11). If you are suffering, don't give up!

Satan

Satan means *adversary*. He is the chief of fallen angels. He hates God and hates God's people. Satan had a very strong hatred for Job and wanted to destroy him. Satan hates any believer who lives totally for God. All of Job's problems can be traced to Satan (chapters 1–2).We must, like Job, take up the "shield of faith" against him (Eph. 6:16; Job 1:20-22; 2:9-10).

Job's wife

Job's wife is a minor character mentioned in 2:9-10. Obviously she suffered because of the loss of her children and because of Job's suffering. However, she had a very negative influence in that she advised Job to "curse God and die!" Her emotions ruled her words.

Eliphaz, Bildad, Zophar

These men were three friends of Job who came to comfort him in his great suffering (2:11-13). Unfortunately, they turned out to be tools of the devil, falsely accusing Job that he suffered because he sinned (chapters 3–31). Be careful what you counsel!

Elihu

Elihu was a young man who sought to help Job when the three other friends became frustrated and gave up (chapters 32–37). He did have some helpful things to tell Job, but it was only God (38:1-42:6) who brought Job back to submission and faith (40:1-5; 42:1-6).

How Does the Story of Job Develop?

The Dramatic Assault of Satan upon God's Servant (1–2)

Are you looking for a hero to admire? Job is your man! In his economic, social, and domestic status, he was the greatest man of the East (1:3). In terms of morality and spirituality, he had no rivals in all the earth (1:1, 8; 2:3).

Satan hated Job. In fact, he hates anyone who lives like Job— "blameless and upright, one who feared God and turned away from evil" (1:1). Satan wants to destroy those whom he hates. Chapters 1–2 record two assaults on Job by Satan (1:6-19; 2:1-8). He accused Job of being a self-centered, selfish hypocrite (1:9-10; 2:4). Job served God for what he could get from Him, said Satan. If God were to remove His favor from Job, Job would curse God to His face (1:11).

> **Our faith can be exceedingly strong even in disaster.**

God allowed Satan to afflict Job severely, taking all his wealth and his children. But instead of cursing God, Job worshiped (1:20-22). Satan attacked again by afflicting Job with a serious and painful disease (2:7-8) but Job still retained his integrity (2:9-10). Satan was wrong about Job. Job did not serve God for gain. Job is a marvelous example from the Old Testament that our faith can be exceedingly strong even in disaster. Faith is not dependent on circumstances. Is this the kind of faith you have?

Three of Job's friends came to comfort him (2:11-13) and were absolutely shocked by what they saw (2:12). They sat with him seven days and seven nights without uttering a word (2:13). Their coming forms the prelude to the next major section of Job (chapters 3–31) in which they seek to help their friend.

Job's Lament and His Debate with the Three Friends (3–31)

This section is tedious for the beginning student studying this great book. It contains Job's lamentation (chapter 3) and a debate between Job and his three friends as to the cause of his sufferings (chapters 4–31).

Seven days and nights of silence end, and Job breaks forth with an anguished cry in which he wishes three things. He wishes he had never been born (3:1-10), he wishes he had died at birth (3:11-19), and he wishes he could now die (3:20-26). For seven days he has struggled over his grief; he cannot reconcile his blameless life with his suffering. Remember that

Job did not know what went on in the heavens when Satan went into the presence of God. The three friends, Eliphaz, Bildad, and Zophar, lacked that information as well.

Chapters 4–31 consist of three cycles of speeches by the friends and Job. Observe how these are laid out:

- *First Cycle (4–14)*. Eliphaz speaks and Job answers in 4–7; Bildad speaks and Job answers in 8–10; Zophar speaks and Job answers in 11–14.
- Second Cycle (15–21). Eliphaz speaks and Job answers in 15–17; Bildad speaks and Job answers in 18–19; Zophar speaks and Job answers in 20–21.
- *Third Cycle (22–31)*. Eliphaz speaks and Job answers in 22–24; Bildad speaks and Job answers in 25–31.

Though Job could not understand why he was suffering, he never once considered that his suffering was because of sin in his life. We know from chapters 1 and 2, of course, that sin was not the problem. However, the three friends persistently accused Job of sin. There was no doubt in their minds that sin was the cause of Job's disaster (see 4:7; 8:6, 20; 11:3-6). Job's suffering would stop only when Job confessed his sin and repented before God (5:8; 8:5-7; 11:13). The three friends grew more dogmatic as the debate continued, and they became exasperated with Job because he would not agree with their interpretation of his tragedy. They thought they had the answers to a problem which in reality they knew nothing about! Their example is a warning to all would be counselors: Counsel on the basis of knowledge and understanding, not preconceived notions or systems.

God wants humble submission to Him in every situation in life.

Job never agreed to their approach to suffering. However, he lost his composure, and in the process of denying that he had sinned, he accused God of being unjust (9:17; 32:2) and unwise (23:3-7; 31:35-37) in handling his painful situation. In the process of all this anger and frustration, Job never lost his positive, long-range trust in God as his Redeemer and Vindicator (19:25). Let us be like Job. Never give up hope no matter how dark the hour. Our Redeemer lives!

But this is not the end of the story. Another person, Elihu, has been listening to the debate. He believes he can help Job where the three friends have failed.

The Intervention of Elihu (32–37)

Elihu was angry. He was angry at the three friends because they condemned Job but had not solved the problem. He was angry with Job because he justified himself at the expense of blaming God (32:23). After Elihu introduced himself (chapter 32), he proceeded to give four messages to which Job did not respond. The first three (chapters 32–35) are similar in form. Elihu made an appeal to listen to him, followed by a quote from Job's speeches to the three, and then he criticized Job's reasoning. The last message (chapters 36–37) is a declaration by Elihu of the righteousness and greatness of God, which Job had doubted.

Were Elihu's messages effective in helping Job? We don't know because Job never responded. Elihu did rebuke Job for his rash words against God during the debate, but he did not fall into the trap of the three friends by blaming Job's problem on some unknown sin. From a positive point of view, Elihu thought suffering was for our discipline and education (33:17-30). Certainly that applied to Job.

We can learn from Elihu. He was a young person who had a burden to help Job, who felt he could make a contribution, and who got involved. Young men and women today can make a difference in the lives of others by following the courageous example of Elihu.

But the story doesn't end with Elihu. It is only God who can help Job in his suffering. Job has been crying out for God to show Himself, and now is the time (chapters 38–42).

God's Dealing with Job and Job's Response (38:1–42:6)

God's dealings with Job are somewhat surprising. We would expect Him to tell Job all that happened in the heavens between God and Satan (chapters 1–2). From what we are told, He never did. God appeared to Job in a storm (38:1; 40:6) signifying that He was coming to judge Job. Judge him for what? For his arrogant, self-justifying accusations against God. Job had said that God was unwise and unjust in His dealings with him. God now holds Job accountable. His judgment is for the purpose of bringing Job back to the kind of submission he had at first (chapters 1–2). It was not so important that Job know *why* he was suffering as it was that he learn *how* to suffer. God wants humble submission to Him in every situation in life.

God's First Approach to Job from the Whirlwind (38:1–40:5)

Job had conveyed that he was wiser than God, so God took the place of the student and told Job to instruct Him (38:3). God questioned Job about the animate and inanimate world. The questions, of course, were intended to humble him. If Job cannot, by his own wisdom, understand the created world, what right does he have to insult the Creator by saying He is unwise! The response from Job is gratifying (40:3-5). He repented and submitted himself to the Lord.

God's Second Approach to Job from the Whirlwind (40:6–42:6)

God spoke again from the whirlwind. This time He took up Job's claim of God's injustice in ruling the world and in ruling Job's life (9:17). So in ironical language, God challenged Job to play God for a day (40:8-14): "Let us see how you will handle the governing of the world." Job must clothe himself with divine attributes and assume divine power (40:9-10). Job was challenged to fulfill the ministry of a judge, of humbling the proud and destroying the wicked. If he could do this successfully, then God would confess that Job is self-sufficient (40:11-14). To narrow it down, God said, "Let's see what you can do with just two animals, the Behemoth (40:15-24) and the Leviathan (41:1-34)." Why, Job doesn't have either the strength or the wisdom to govern these two animals, let alone the universe. Job's inability to govern the universe makes him inadequate and unqualified to criticize God's actions as ruler either of the universe or of Job personally (9:17). Job had no righteous grounds, then, to call God's justice into question. The response from Job was once again gratifying (42:1-6). He repented and submitted to the Lord. His trial was over, and now it was time for restoration.

Conclusion to the Story of Job (42:7-17)

Everyone loves a story that ends well. The book of Job ends with God rebuking the three friends and making provision for their restoration (42:79). Though God was angry with the friends, He loved them and wanted them reconciled to Himself and to Job.

Job's prosperity was restored "when he had prayed for his friends." He received twice as much as before except for the number of his children. The author of Job recorded that Job's relatives and friends returned as well when they learned about Job's new prosperity (40:10-17).

We are glad that God honored Job with this return of fortune, but we must remember that God nowhere promises this to the Christian who suffers some kind of loss. If He does, praise Him for it. If He does not, praise Him still.

LESSON 1 EXAM

Use the exam sheet that has been provided to complete your exam.

1. **The Old Testament is made up of**
    A. 23 books.   C. 32 books.
    B. 27 books.   D. 39 books.

2. **In synonymous parallelism**
    A. the second line is in contrast to the first.
    B. the second line is the same thought as the first.
    C. the second line adds something to the first.
    D. the second line is an illustration of the first.

3. **Job is a long book consisting of**
    A. 22 chapters.   C. 42 chapters.
    B. 32 chapters.   D. 52 chapters.

4. **The events of Job probably took place during the time of**
    A. the patriarchs.
    B. the Egyptian bondage.
    C. the judges' period.
    D. the kings' period.

5. **Job was a genuine character of history as evidenced in**
    A. Isaiah and Matthew.
    B. Jeremiah and Romans.
    C. Ezekiel and James.
    D. Daniel and Revelation.

6. **Satan's first assault was against**
    A. Job's person.
    B. Job's possessions and children.
    C. Job's wife.
    D. Job's three friends.

7. **Chapters 4-31 contain**
    A. two cycles of debate.
    B. three cycles of debate.
    C. four cycles of debate.
    D. five cycles of debate.

8. **In chapters 4-31, Job's three friends explained his suffering as**
    A. the result of Job's sin.
    B. the work of Satan.
    C. God's love in disguise.
    D. an act of fate.

9. **What was Elihu's view of Job's suffering?**
    A. Job had suffered for some unknown sin.
    B. Job had not sinned at all.
    C. The three friends were correct in their evaluation.
    D. Job's sufferings were disciplinary and educational.

10. **Job accused God during his debate with the three of being**
    A. unwise and unjust.
    B. unloving.
    C. unfaithful to His promises.
    D. callous to his pain.

What Do You Say?

What have you discovered in the Bible about suffering that has been helpful to you?

Psalms: Part One

Prayer and Worship to our God

The Psalms have been a magnificent source of inspiration, encouragement, and spiritual insight for God's people throughout the centuries. Though the book of Psalms is old, it is ever new. Its vast range of topics, its variety of life experiences, and its practical insights on man's relationship with God and with one another are as appropriate today as in Old Testament days. Let us then survey the Psalms with the attitude that this could be the beginning of a lifetime of study and meditation which could result in a deep and worshipful walk with God.

God's mercy rescues His own from trouble and disaster.

Psalms was the national hymnbook for Israel. It is devoted to prayer and praise to our God. If prayer and praise are characteristic of your life, then you will enjoy Psalms. If not, then this study may challenge you to make them a priority!

The many authors who contributed their poems for this national hymnbook knew God in a very personal way. When we read their works we can sense their devotion to Him. They celebrated the great person and work of our God. He is a loving God who tenderly shepherds His people (Ps. 23). He is a protecting God who is "our refuge and strength, a very present help in trouble" (Ps. 46). He is a delivering God who in His mercy rescues His own from trouble and disaster (Ps. 3). He is a sovereign God who has decreed that His Son, the Messiah, will reign over the earth (Ps. 2:6-8). He is an all-powerful God (Ps. 2:9) who by His might will smash the rebellion of men and establish the rule of His Son upon the throne of David. He is an all-wise God (Ps. 119) who has provided wisdom for His people through His blessed Word. He is the ever-present God who knows our every situation in life (Ps. 139:1-12). He is the merciful God who delights to forgive His falling and fallen people and restore them to fellowship with Himself and others

(Ps. 32, 51). He is a holy God and "holy and awesome is His name" (Ps. 89:18; 111:9). In His holiness, He is above and beyond and separate from His creatures and creation. He is supremely majestic! Let us with the psalmist of ancient days "Give unto the LORD the glory due to His name" and let us "ascribe to the LORD the glory due his name; worship the Lord in the splendor of holiness" (Ps. 29:2).

The Number of Psalms

There are 150 psalms in the book of Psalms. That makes it the longest book in the Bible. Individual psalms vary in length. Psalm 119 has 176 verses in contrast to Psalm 117 which has only two. Though the book of Psalms is long, it is very practical and rewarding to those who take the time to read and meditate on it.

The Division of the Psalms

Psalms is divided into five distinct books. Most modern translations indicate this. These divisions are laid out as follows:

Book one	Psalms 1-41
Book two	Psalms 42-72
Book three	Psalms 73-89
Book four	Psalms 90-106
Book five	Psalms 107-150

Each of these "books" ends with a doxology (praise) to God. Read these verses (41:13; 72:18-19; 89:52; 106:48; 150:1-6) so you can discern the emphasis.

Scholars have puzzled over the reason for these divisions. Some have thought that the five books correspond to the first five books of the Bible—Genesis, Exodus, Leviticus, Numbers, and Deuteronomy. That is, when the book of Genesis was read in the synagogue service, Book One of the Psalms was read with it. Not knowing the exact reason for the five divisions does not spoil our appreciation for this great inspirational book. Read it with delight!

The Period of the Psalms

The book of Psalms was written over a long period of time. That period stretched from Moses through David to Ezra.

Moses 16th-15th centuries BC.	**David** 11th-10th centuries BC.	**Ezra** 5th century BC.

Moses wrote Psalm 90, David wrote seventy-three psalms, and Ezra, according to some, wrote Psalm 119. There were several other composers (see the psalm titles), but David wrote the most psalms. He contributed close to half of the total. Many of David's psalms arose from his personal experiences (Psalms 3, 32, 51), but some of them (Psalms 2, 110) were purely prophetic of the coming Messiah, Jesus Christ.

The Formation of the Book of Psalms

How did the book of Psalms get into its present five-fold division of 150 psalms? Note the following theory:

- *Step One:* Individual psalms were written from time to time without any thought of creating a collection.
- *Step Two:* These individual psalms were collected at various times and put into small collections. There is evidence in the Book of Psalms of the existence of small collections. Note the following illustrations:

Psalms of Ascents	120-134
Praise Psalms	146-150
David's Psalms	1-41 (and others)

- *Step Three:* The small collections were gathered by someone (Ezra?) for the purpose of putting them into one big collection.
- *Step Four:* The final work of choosing and arranging was then done as guided and inspired by the Holy Spirit.

The above process would be somewhat parallel to compiling a modern hymnbook for use in Christian worship.

Types of Psalms in the Book of Psalms

Variety is the spice of life, and the book of Psalms has abundant variety! The following are some samples of the various categories of psalms and are not intended to be exhaustive.

Wisdom Psalms (1, 73, 112, 127)

Wisdom in the Old Testament was not philosophical speculation. It was the Word of God—divine revelation. To the Old Testament believer, wisdom was the greatest thing one could possess (see Prov. 3:13-20; 4:5-19; 8:1-36). Solomon said that the fear of the Lord is the beginning of wisdom (Prov. 1:7). There is more emphasis in Proverbs on wisdom, but Psalms includes some as well.

Wisdom psalms focus primarily on two important questions:

1. What is the relationship between godliness and reward?
2. How does God deal with people who sin?

These are questions asked by thinking people in any age. Psalm 73 is one of the classic answers to these questions.

Penitential Psalms (6, 32, 38, 51, 102, 130)

These are psalms of sorrow over, and repentance from, sin. Psalms 32 and 51 are the most notable ones in the experience of David. The background for these psalms is 2 Samuel 11–12. Read them and thank God for His mercy and love.

Praise Psalms (146–150)

This group of psalms (and there are others) emphasizes praise from start to finish. Praise emphasizes the person of God, whereas thanksgiving stresses His benefits. Praise celebrates who God is and what He has done. Learning to praise God is a mark of growth and maturity.

Petition Psalms (3–4)

These are psalms in which the psalmist has a problem or is in some kind of trouble. Instead of giving up he calls upon God to deliver him. We can all identify with this kind of situation. David had many such problems, and we will be greatly blessed to see how he trusted God.

Historical Psalms (78, 105, 106, 135, 136)

Various parts of the history of Israel are traced in these psalms. For instance, Psalm 105 traces Israel's history from Abraham to the taking of the land of Canaan. What is the psalmist's purpose? It is not only to give us a history lesson, but also to emphasize God's faithfulness to His promise. Psalm 106 traces Israel's history from Egypt to the Babylonian captivity. Why? It is to emphasize God's mercy to Israel in the face of their constant sin and rebellion. History can teach us some valuable lessons if we are willing to learn!

Messianic Psalms (2, 16, 22, 40, 69, 110, 118)

A *messianic psalm* is a prophecy either in part or in whole of the coming Messiah. Psalm 110 is an example of a messianic psalm which speaks only of the Messiah; it presents Jesus as King, Priest, and Judge. The New Testament refers to these psalms several times.

Psalm 16 is an example of a partially messianic psalm. The latter part of the psalm (16:8-11) refers exclusively to Jesus Christ, not to David. Peter quotes these verses in the book of Acts (2:25-28) as referring to the body of the resurrected Lord Jesus Christ which did not undergo decay. (Some Bible students believe verses 8-11 also refer to David in a lesser way.)

> **A messianic psalm is a prophecy of the coming Messiah.**

Jesus taught that not only the Law and the Prophets but also the book of Psalms spoke prophetically of Him (Luke 24:44). It is a fact that the Psalms trace the career of our Lord from eternity to eternity. We will note this in *Part Two* of our survey of the Psalms.

Pilgrimage Psalms

These psalms (120–134) are sometimes called "songs of degrees" or "songs of ascent." As pilgrims made their way to Jerusalem to celebrate the various holy days, they would sing these songs as they ascended to the holy city.

The subject matter of psalms is varied and includes prayer, petition, praise, and thanksgiving. There is through all of them the element of trust in a good and faithful God.

It is good on any day, not just Sundays, to have a song of praise in our hearts wherever we go. Paul tells us that one of the evidences of being filled with the Spirit is "addressing one another in psalms and hymns and spiritual songs, singing and making melody to the Lord with your heart" (Eph. 5:19).

LESSON 2 EXAM

Use the exam sheet that has been provided to complete your exam.

1. **The book of Psalms consists of 150 psalms arranged in**
   A. three divisions.
   B. five divisions.
   C. seven divisions.
   D. eight divisions.

2. **Each of the major divisions of the Psalms closes with**
   A. a doxology.
   B. a petition.
   C. an exhortation.
   D. a warning.

3. **The period covered by Psalms stretched from**
   A. Adam to Solomon.
   B. Abraham to Hezekiah.
   C. Moses to Ezra.
   D. David to Malachi.

4. **A *Penitential Psalm* is a psalm of**
   A. sorrow over, and repentance from, sin.
   B. praise for who God is.
   C. request for deliverance from trouble.
   D. some aspect of Israel's history.

5. **A psalm which focuses on the relationship between godliness and reward is a**
   A. messianic psalm.
   B. historical psalm.
   C. petition psalm.
   D. wisdom psalm.

6. **The composer of most of the Psalms was**
   A. Solomon.   C. David.
   B. Hezekiah.   D. Ezra.

7. **One illustration of the existence of small collections of psalms in the book of Psalms is**
   A. psalms of praise.   C. psalms of holiness.
   B. psalms of wrath.   D. psalms of sorrow.

8. **One Messianic Psalm which speaks only of the Messiah is**
   A. Psalm 1.   C. Psalm 73.
   B. Psalm 29.   D. Psalm 110.

9. **Many of David's psalms arose from**
   A. his poetic genius.
   B. his personal experience.
   C. his theological discussions.
   D. his consultation with others.

10. **A psalm which tells us how God deals with people who sin is a**
    A. penitential psalm.
    B. petition psalm.
    C. wisdom psalm.
    D. historical psalm.

EXAM 2

What Do You Say?

What is your favorite type of psalm and why?

Psalms: Part Two

Psalm Forms

The Psalms are also varied in the way in which the writers constructed their poems. Most readers do not approach reading Psalms with this in mind. Let's observe some of the structures of selected psalms.

The Contrastive Psalm (Ps. 1)

This is a psalm which forms a contrast all the way through. Observe how this works in Psalm 1:

- *Two groups* — the godly (blessed man) and the ungodly (1:1-3)
- *Two guides* — the Law of the Lord (1:2) and the counsel of the ungodly (1:1)
- *Two Characters* — the fruitful for God (1:3) and the worthless to God (1:4)
- *Two Destinies* — the godly approved (1:6) and the ungodly disapproved (1:5-6)

This psalm is appropriate to begin the whole book because it states the general principles for godly living that are constantly emphasized in the rest of the psalms.

The Petition Psalm (Ps. 3)

This is a psalm in which the psalmist is in some kind of trouble. He seeks help from God and is delivered. In Psalm 3, David's troubles were severe (3:1-2), but God was greater than his troubles and sufficient for his situation (3:3-4). Thus, he could be at peace with the confidence that God would deliver him (3:5-7). He closed the psalm with a benediction (3:8).

This is a psalm we can live by! When we are in trouble and tempted to give up, let us remember that God is able to help us.

The Dramatic Psalm (Ps. 2 and others)

This is a psalm which dramatizes an event or situation using several different speakers. Observe the layout of Psalm 2 which has as its theme the future reign of the Messiah.

1. *The First Speaker (2:1-2).* The psalmist speaks telling of a conspiracy against the Lord and His anointed one (Jesus).
2. *The Second Speaker (2:3).* The conspirators speak revealing their plan to deliver themselves from all divine restraint.
3. *The Third Speaker (2:4-5).* The psalmist speaks, telling of God's intervention in wrath against puny humans who would dare to rebel against Him.
4. *The Fourth Speaker (2:6).* The Lord speaks. He will see to it that His rejected Son reigns!
5. *The Fifth Speaker (2:7-9).* Jesus speaks quoting His Father. He tells us that God the Father has decreed that He shall reign.
6. *The Sixth Speaker (2:10-12).* The psalmist speaks by applying the psalm to the rulers of his own day. They should submit to God!

What a thrilling psalm this is! We can take heart in the fact that our God is in control. Nothing can stop His plan to establish His Son upon the throne of David! We should heed the warning of the psalmist to submit to the Son of God as Lord of our lives. Truly, "Blessed are all who take refuge in him" (2:12).

The Repetitive Psalm (Ps. 107)

The repetitive psalm form states a theme (or themes) and then constantly reworks and illustrates it throughout the psalm. Psalm 107 has two themes. The first is the goodness of God (107:1-32), and the second the government of God (107:33-43).

The *goodness of God* is announced in the introduction (Ps. 107:1-3). Then the psalmist proceeds to describe four adverse situations in which the goodness of God is shown to His afflicted people.

- Lost in the desert (107:4-9)
- Locked in the dungeon (107:10-16)

- Lying on a death bed (107:7-22)
- Suffering weakness and hardship at sea (107:23-32)

Each of these adverse situations has the following pattern which you should take time to discover:

- The problem stated (as seen above)
- The prayer for deliverance
- The intervention of God
- Thanksgiving for His goodness

The *government of God* refers to His rule over creation. God's rule is manifested in His person and attributes. He rules the world with wisdom, providence, sovereignty, power, justice, holiness, and love. Observe the alternating pattern of God's rule as developed by the psalmist:

1. Punishment (107:33-34)
2. Prosperity (107:35-38)
3. Punishment (107:39-40)
4. Prosperity (107:41-42)

Just as we can trust God's goodness (107:1-32), so we can trust His rule (107:33-43). People who have a worldly view have left God out of their thinking. They are foolish. The psalmist concludes by teaching that whoever is wise will see the hand of God behind the events of earth and will understand the loving kindness of God (107:43). Let us then interpret the events of our lives, good or bad, as under God's control and care (Job 2:10).

The Conclusion-Didactic Psalm (Ps. 32)

This is a psalm form in which the author has come to some conclusion in his life. He states that conclusion at the beginning of the psalm and then proceeds to tell the route he took in arriving at it. He ends with an application. Observe how this works for Psalm 32, a psalm of David.

- *The Conclusion:* David came to the conclusion through his experience that the happy person is the forgiven person (32:1-2).
- *The Route:* First there was a period of silence (32:3a) when he was hiding his sin. This was followed by a period of severe chastisement (32:3b-4) that led to acknowledging and confessing his sin (32:5).

- *Application:* David tells how other sinners can have the security and peace that come through forgiveness (32:6-7). He instructs as to how we can maintain constant fellowship with God through knowledge (32:8), submission (32:9), trust (32:10), and joy (32:11).

The Alphabetical Psalm (Ps. 119)

This is a psalm which forms an alphabetical acrostic. Psalm 119 is the most outstanding of these. It has twenty-two sections based on the twenty-two letters of the Hebrew alphabet. Each of the twenty-two sections has eight verses. Each of the first eight verses begins with the Hebrew letter *aleph*, the next eight with the second Hebrew letter *beth*, and so on through the psalm. Most modern English translations of the Bible indicate the alphabetic divisions.

We need to fill our minds with God's holy Word!

We do not know for certain why this literary form was used. Some scholars think it was to make the memorization of the psalm easier. The subject of Psalm 119 is the incredible importance of the Word of God, so it is a psalm worth memorizing! We need to fill our minds with God's holy Word! God uses His Word to shape and mold our thinking so as to develop our spiritual lives in His image.

There are other psalm forms, but these six will give you an idea of the fascinating variety in their compositions.

Jesus Christ in the Book of Psalms

Jesus said that the psalms spoke of Him (Luke 24:44). Observe the very clear evidence of this in chart form:

Jesus Christ	Psalms	New Testament References
His Eternity	102:25-27	Hebrews 1:10-12
His Deity	45:6	Hebrews 1:8
Descended from David	89:3-4, 28-29, 34-36; 132:11-12	Acts 2:30
Incarnation	40:6-8	Hebrews 10:5-10
Humiliation	8:4	Hebrews 2:6

Jesus Crhist	Psalms	New Testament References
Ministry	69:9	John 2:17
Parabolic Teaching	78:2	Matthew 13:35
Rejection	118:22	Matthew 21:42
Betrayal	41:9	John 13:18
Crucifixion	22	Matthew 27:46
Hatred	69:4	John 15:25
Given sour wine	69:21	Matthew 27:34
Reproaches	69:9b	Romans 15:3
No Corruption	16:10	Acts 2:24-31
Resurrection	16:9-11	Acts 2:26-28
Appearances	22:22	Hebrews 2:12
Ascension	68:18	Ephesians 4:8-10
Ascension and Priesthood	110	Matthew 22:43-45; Acts 2:33-35; Hebrews 1:13; 5:6-10; 6:20; 7:24
His Throne	45:6a	Hebrews 1:8-9
His Rule	2:8-9	Revelation 2:26-27; 12:5; 19:15

LESSON 3 EXAM

Use the exam sheet that has been provided to complete your exam.

1. **The contrastive psalm was illustrated by**
   A. Psalm 1.   C. Psalm 42.
   B. Psalm 13.   D. Psalm 57.

2. **A psalm in which the psalmist is in some kind of trouble and seeks help from God is a**
   A. petition psalm.
   B. dramatic psalm.
   C. repetitive psalm.
   D. didactic psalm.

3. **The theme of Psalm 2, a dramatic psalm form, is**
   A. the cross of Jesus.
   B. the life of Jesus.
   C. the teaching of Jesus.
   D. the reign of Jesus.

4. **The dramatic psalm form is one that**
   A. has several speakers.
   B. begins with a conclusion.
   C. forms a contrast all the way through.
   D. has a theme which is constantly repeated.

5. **Psalm 107 has two themes. They are**
   A. the wisdom and power of God.
   B. the goodness and government of God.
   C. the holiness and wrath of God.
   D. the omnipresence and love of God.

6. **The conclusion-didactic psalm was illustrated by**
   A. Psalm 23.   C. Psalm 37.
   B. Psalm 32.   D. Psalm 103.

7. **Psalm 107 is a good example of the**
   A. alphabetical psalm.
   B. repetitive psalm.
   C. dramatic psalm.
   D. contrastive psalm.

8. **Psalm 119, an alphabetical psalm, has as its subject**
   A. worship.
   B. witnessing.
   C. personal relationships.
   D. the Word of God.

9. **Some speculate that the alphabetic literary form was used to**
   A. teach children the alphabet.
   B. make memorization easier.
   C. show the fullness of God's revelation.
   D. be a type of Jesus Christ.

10. **References to Jesus in the Psalms begin with His**
    A. incarnation and end with His death.
    B. ministry and end with His resurrection.
    C. rejection and end with His ascension.
    D. eternity and end with His rule.

What Do You Say?

What psalm would you use to help a "worldly" young person, and why?

Proverbs, Ecclesiastes, and The Song of Solomon

PROVERBS

Wise Living on Earth in the Fear of God

We live in a world that desperately needs the wisdom found in the book of Proverbs. Young people especially need it. In fact, Proverbs is primarily addressed to them. In the first nine chapters, Solomon, who contributed most of the book, addressed his wisdom fifteen times to his son. It isn't that older people cannot benefit from Proverbs; they can and should. Solomon made it clear that the "wise" person (1:5) wasn't beyond the need to learn and apply the teachings of this book. However, young people are especially open to many influences—both good and bad. They need practical wisdom (1:4) to shape and mold their young lives, setting them on a course that will build character in their relationship with God and others.

Wisdom in the Old Testament

But what is wisdom in the Old Testament? First, it is not philosophical speculation on life, as taught by the ancient Greeks. Nor is it related to being very intelligent. Wisdom in Proverbs and throughout the Old Testament is very practical. It is developed out of the experience and activity of humankind. That experience is then distilled or capsulized into principles for living.

The word "wisdom" (*hokmak* in Hebrew) basically means to have a skill. It describes those who skillfully made the various parts of the tabernacle (Ex. 36:1-8). Jeremiah 10:9 uses it to describe one who was skillful as a goldsmith. It describes Joseph, who had governmental skills (Gen. 41:39), and Solomon, who had judicial skills (1 Kings 3:28; 4:29). In Proverbs, wisdom is skill in one's relationship with God and man.

The way of wisdom is the way of honesty, uprightness, purity, and discipline. The artistic skill of Aholiab and Bezaleel helped them create beautiful works of art (Ex. 28:3; 36:1-8). In the same way, the wisdom of the Book of Proverbs gives us the ability to make our lives beautiful for God and useful to man.

> **The person who will benefit from the wisdom found in Proverbs is the one who trusts the source of all true wisdom—God.**

The person who will benefit from the wisdom found in Proverbs is the one who trusts the source of all true wisdom—God. Solomon wrote the "fear of the LORD is the beginning of wisdom, and the knowledge of the Holy One is insight" (9:10). He also wrote that "fools despise wisdom and instruction" (1:7). The "fool" in the book of Proverbs is not necessarily slow mentally. In fact, he may be very smart. The fool in Proverbs is morally, religiously, and spiritually bankrupt. He has no time for God and does not want God to reign over his life. Psalm 14:1 speaks of the fool as an atheist: "The fool says in his heart, 'There is no God.'" Solomon challenges us to go seek wisdom (4:5-7). He says that if we "prize her" we can expect exaltation, honor, grace, and beauty (4:8-9). What more could one desire from God?

The Word "Proverb" (from the Hebrew word *mashal*)

Scholars have debated the meaning of the Hebrew word translated by our English word "proverb." Most think it means something like "to be like," which would involve a comparison. Whatever the original meaning, it is clear that proverbs are experiences intended to instruct young men and women.

This word *mashal* is used either of a discourse or an aphorism in the book of Proverbs. While a discourse might be a long discussion on a topic, an aphorism is a short pithy sentence which states a truth: "A soft answer turns away wrath, but a harsh word stirs up anger" (15:1). One does not need to be a genius to understand the point. Like most of the proverbs, the truth is right on the surface!

Mashal is used in even greater variety outside Proverbs. For example, Ezekiel uses it of allegory (17:2), Micah of a lament (2:4), and the book of Numbers of a prophetic discourse (23:7; 24:15).

The Purpose of the Book of Proverbs

Proverbs 1:2-6 sets forth the purpose for which the book was written. Verse 2 summarizes the purpose: "To know wisdom and instruction, to understand words of insight." Verses 3 and 4 then amplify the first part of this summary verse. In verse 3 it is from the perspective of the student—what he shall receive. In verse 4 it is from the perspective of the teacher—what he shall give. Verse 5 says that though the book is primarily for the young, the mature will benefit. Verse 6 closes the purpose statement and expands the summary statement of verse 2: "To understand words of insight." Observe this in chart form:

Summary of the Purpose	2 To know wisdom and instruction; to understand words of insight,
Amplification: First Part of Summary Verse	3 to receive instruction in wise dealing, in righteousness, justice, and equity; 4 to give prudence to the simple, knowledge and discretion to the youth—
Parenthetical Clarification	5 Let the wise hear and increase in learning, and the one who understands obtain guidance,
Amplification: Second part of summary verse	6 to understand a proverb and a saying, the words of the wise and their riddles.

Thus we learn from this purpose statement that the book of Proverbs intends to teach us. Proverbs focuses on teaching wisdom rather than arguing a particular point of view. If you want to be successful in life in relation to God and man, then read, believe, and practice the wisdom of Proverbs. That means you may read a chapter a day and complete the book in a thirty-one-day month. If you find verses that apply to your situation in life, commit them to memory. Then review them from time to time and share them with others for their blessing and benefit.

The Structure of the Book of Proverbs

I	II	III	IV
The proverbs of Solomon 1:1-22:16	The proverbs of the wise 22:17-24:34	The proverbs of Solomon 25-29	The proverbs of Lemuel & Agur 30-31

The structure is formed on the basis of those who contributed to the book of Proverbs.

Solomon

Solomon is without doubt the one responsible for composing most of the proverbs in the book (1:1; 10:1; 25:1). 1 Kings 4:32 tells us that Solomon spoke three thousand proverbs. However, God has preserved only a small portion of these. God greatly gifted Solomon with wisdom (1 Kings 3). We can benefit greatly from that wisdom. It is unfortunate that later in his life Solomon no longer took his own wise advice! His failure did not make his great writings any less true or useful. We can still learn much from everything he wrote and pray that God will preserve us from the same mistakes.

The Wise

Scholars tell us that the term "the wise" (22:17; 24:23) is a technical term for groups of men who gave themselves to the pursuit of wisdom. One theory is that these men were non-Israelites who lived before Solomon's time. Solomon was familiar with their wisdom, collected it, and chose certain of their proverbs as a part of the book.

Lemuel and Agur

The identity of these men is unknown.

The Subject Matter of the Book of Proverbs

Proverbs is packed full of practical topics dealing with everyday living: peer pressure, sexual purity, sound business practices, disciplined living, self-control, family relations, social relations, generosity, the use of the tongue, the pursuit of wisdom, kindness, marriage, thrift, wine, work, anger, friendships, wealth, and many more. Although the book is relevant for people of all ages, Proverbs was written to guide and restrain youth who are bombarded daily with temptations!

ECCLESIASTES

True Meaning and Joy of Life

Ecclesiastes is probably one of the least read books of the Old Testament. Maybe this is so because it is philosophical in nature. It requires thoughtful meditation to understand the author's perspective and purpose in writing. Try reading this book of wisdom at one sitting. As you read, observe words, phrases, and ideas that occur often. Only the careful and diligent student of Ecclesiastes will gain insight and satisfaction.

The Title of the Book

To most people, *Ecclesiastes* is a strange title for a book of the Bible. What does it mean? Ecclesiastes is a Greek word which has been transliterated into English. Transliteration is (in this instance) the assigning of equivalent English letters to the Greek letters. The word means "the preacher" (1:1), one who assembles God's people to teach or proclaim God's truth.

The Author of the Book—King Solomon

The "Preacher" does not give his name in the book. He describes himself as the "son of David, king of Israel" (1:1, 12) and as a "wise man" (12:9) who taught the people wisdom. Though not all scholars agree who the author is, the author of this study assumes that Solomon wrote the book. Solomon had the background, credentials, and experiences needed to write Ecclesiastes. He had massive wealth, lots of time, great intelligence, and incredible wisdom. Jewish tradition attributed the authorship to Solomon. Most conservative Christian scholars agree.

Background Leading Up to Writing Ecclesiastes

Surveying the life of Solomon will help us understand why he wrote Ecclesiastes.

Solomon's Prayer (1 Kings 3)

Solomon, a true believer, asked God in deep humility for wisdom to guide the kingdom. God not only gave him his request but also added the promise of great wealth.

Solomon's Prosperity and Power (1 Kings 4-10)

These chapters illustrate the greatness of Solomon's wealth and wisdom. However, during the last 20 years of his reign he began to move away from God. This happened when he married more foreign wives, who brought with them their idols (1 Kings 11:1-3).

Solomon's Sin and Degradation (1 Kings 11)

This chapter pictures the depth of Solomon's sin. He had a spiritually divided heart which stamped its image on the kingdom. He caused religious, social, and political division in the nation. His rebellion and insensitivity toward God made God remote in his daily life. He was frustrated, unhappy, and desperately searching for what was really important in life (Eccl. 1-2). He was like someone trying to complete a 500-piece puzzle without first making the border! God rebuked Solomon (11:9-11) and told him of severe chastisement to come.

Solomon's Search and Recovery (Eccl. 1-2)

The author of this study believes that Solomon responded in a positive way to God's rebuke and discipline (1 Kings 11). Ecclesiastes 1-2 gives testimony to that fact. In these chapters Solomon tells of the frustrating search he made trying to get meaning and purpose back in his life. He couldn't find it by human wisdom or in a self-centered and indulgent lifestyle. He found it in getting back to God! In 2:24-26 he summarizes his renewed faith. He testifies that even in the very mundane things of life—eating, drinking, and laboring—one cannot be truly content without God!

Solomon's Basic Perspective

Ecclesiastes 12:13-14 states clearly Solomon's godly perspective as he concludes his book: "The end of the matter; all has been heard. *Fear God and keep His commandments*, for this is the whole duty of man. For God will bring every deed into judgment, with every secret thing, whether good or evil." These two verses tell us that Solomon believed in God and that God should be feared (that is, reverenced). We must keep His Word, for a day is coming when everyone must give account to Him who will judge every act. This is an awesome thought, and one that should make us sensitive to God's claims on our lives.

Recurring Phrases and Ideas in Ecclesiastes

There are several of these, but let us look at just a few of the more important ones:

Vanity of Vanities (1:2)

First impressions tend to dominate. Since 1:1–1-2 illustrates the vanity of life, the reader might think that this is what all of Ecclesiastes is about. The point Solomon wants to make is that life is indeed vain (empty) if one leaves God out of his life (as Solomon had done). Your world view will determine how you look at life. If your world view does not include God, then life does not have anything worth valuing.

Under the Sun (1:3)

This is a neutral term. It simply means "on earth." One either lives his life "under the sun" as a believer or an unbeliever!

Eating and Drinking (2:24-26)

There are several of these eating and drinking passages. Some have interpreted them in an Epicurean sense, that is, "Eat, drink, and be merry, for tomorrow we die." But Solomon never recommends that. Paul says that "God … provides us with everything to enjoy" (1 Tim. 6:17). Solomon is telling us that giving God the proper place in our lives transforms even the most common things of life (2:24).

The Structure of Ecclesiastes

The structure of Ecclesiastes is built around the theme of the book which is *knowing the true meaning in life through knowing God.*

1. Introduction—Vanity of Vanities (1:1-11)
2. The Search for True Meaning in Life (1:12-2:26)
3. The Basis for True Meaning in Life (3:1-5:20)
4. The Clarification of True Meaning in Life (6:1-8:15)
5. The Application of True Meaning in Life (8:16-12:8)
6. Conclusion—Fear God and Keep His Word (12:9-14)

When we know the true meaning of life through knowing God, we can expect God's incredible joy in all areas of life.

THE SONG OF SOLOMON

"I Am my Beloved's and my Beloved is Mine"

In a day when faithfulness in marriage is at an all time low, there is a great need to rediscover the truths of the "Song of Songs, which is Solomon's" (1:1). Solomon wrote over a thousand songs (1 Kings 4:32) and this one, by its title, is declared to be the best. It is a song of love between two people who are unconditionally committed to one another. In one sense, the Song of Solomon explains God's original intention in love and marriage as declared in Genesis 2:24-25: "Therefore a man shall leave his father and his mother and hold fast to his wife, and they shall become one flesh. And the man and his wife were both naked and were not ashamed." These verses teach us that marriage is an exclusive relationship (shall leave), a permanent relationship (be joined, or cleave), a unified relationship (shall become one flesh), and a harmonious relationship (both naked and were not ashamed). In Solomon's day many men took several wives, a severe departure from God's original intention. The Song of Solomon was written to correct that problem. It is needed today as well!

The Author—Solomon

There is no doubt that Solomon was the author of this book. The first verse (1:1) tells us this, and he is mentioned throughout the Song (1:5; 3:7,

9, 11; 8:11). He was king in Jerusalem at the time (see 3:6-11) with a harem of sixty queens and eighty concubines (6:8). 1 Kings 11:3 relates that at the end of his life he had "700 wives ... and 300 concubines." He wrote this song in spite of his own miserable failure in love and marriage so that Israel might have a drama describing what a biblical love relationship is. It was not unusual for biblical writers to compose writings which were unflattering to themselves. David wrote Psalms 32 and 51 which reflect his own adultery and murder.

The Interpretation of the Song

Many of the ancient interpreters of the Song were embarrassed by the vivid sexual descriptions in it (4:1-6; 7:1-9) and so looked upon it as an allegory tracing the history of Israel from the exodus from Egypt to the coming of the Messiah. Jewish people read the Song at Passover.

Some modern interpreters view the Song of Solomon as a group of love poems compiled in a book to be used at wedding services. In this view the poems have no relationship to one another and thus they tell no unified story. It would be like getting a number of your favorite poems together and compiling them in an album or book. One reading of the Song of Solomon will demonstrate that this is not the correct approach.

> **Songs of Salomon is a literal, actual love story composed in poetic language.**

Most modern conservative scholars interpret the song as a *literal, actual love story* composed in poetic language. It is the story of two people who are unconditionally committed to one another in keeping with God's original design revealed in Genesis 2:24-25. The young woman of the Song is called the Shulamite (6:13). She is very beautiful and virtuous. The young man of the Song is often called the "beloved" (2:8). Is there a clear identity for this man? No. Some interpreters identify him with Solomon while others believe he is an unnamed shepherd who is the fiancé of the Shulamite. If Solomon is the beloved, then the story centers on the courtship and marriage of the two. If the shepherd is the beloved, then the story views Solomon in a negative way. In this interpretation the Shulamite was brought to Solomon's palace against her will. Solomon sought to woo her away from her beloved shepherd fiancé. He was unsuccessful, and she was allowed to return to her beloved. When she returned they renewed their commitment to one another (8:6). The Shulamite took the initiative, asking for a pledge from her beloved. "Set me as a seal upon your heart, as a seal upon your arm, for love is strong as death, jealousy is fierce as the grave. Its flashes are flashes of fire, the very flame of the LORD."

Application of the Song

There is disagreement among bible scholars as to the identity of the "beloved," but that should not hinder us from enjoying the drama and finding in it application for our lives. Observe just a few of these.

The Appeal of Love

The Shulamite called to her beloved, "Set me as a seal upon your heart, as a seal upon your arm" (8:6a). The heart stands for affection and the arm for strength. She wants the continued love of his heart and the protection and security that come from his strength. This is what Boaz gave to Ruth in their relationship (Ruth 4). Good relationships in courtship and marriage should have these ingredients.

The Power of Love

The Shulamite said that "love is strong as death" (8:6b). Love and death have one thing in common. They are both irresistible forces once they take hold of man. Paul says that "God's love has been poured into our hearts through the Holy Spirit who has been given to us" (Rom. 5:5). We can love supernaturally in any relationship because God has given us His gift of love. We must remember, however, that the love within us has to be nurtured and developed in our relationships.

The Endurance of Love

"Many waters cannot quench love, neither can floods drown it" (8:7a). Genuine love cannot be destroyed. Love can endure all kinds of assaults. Paul said that "love ... endures all things" and that "love never ends" (1 Cor. 13:7-8). May that quality of endurance be manifested in our lives throughout our total life on earth.

The Pricelessness of Love

"If a man offered for love all the wealth of his house, he would be utterly despised" (8:7b). Attempts to buy affection through wealth, flattery, and sensuous appeals deserve to fail. Genuine love cannot be bought! It was while we were yet sinners, not saints, that God showed His love to us in the giving of Jesus Christ to be our Savior (John 3:16; Rom. 5:8). We were morally, religiously, and spiritually bankrupt, having nothing to give to obtain our salvation.

The Exclusiveness of Love

The Shulamite said, "My beloved is mine, and I am his" (2:16a). They only had eyes for one another. She belonged to him and he to her. This is what God intended when He created marriage in Genesis 2:24-25. The believer in Jesus has the same kind of exclusive relationship to Him in the spiritual sense. The New Testament pictures the church as the bride and Jesus Christ as the bridegroom (Eph. 5:22-27).

Because of the intimate language of the Song, there was a Jewish saying that said that the Song should not be studied by anyone until he was thirty years of age. However, married love with all its physical and emotional beauty was ordained of God, and we should not be embarrassed to understand it. We should teach our children from an early age about married love and the responsibilities that go along with it. Christians do not need to leave this kind of training to the public school system. Also, children should be warned about the distortion and exploitation of the erotic nature of love by the publishers and peddlers of pornography.

LESSON 4 EXAM

Use the exam sheet that has been provided to complete your exam.

1. **Wisdom in the book of Proverbs basically means**
   A. philosophical speculation.
   B. a skill.
   C. high intelligence.
   D. great knowledge.

2. **The word *proverb* means**
   A. "to be like."
   B. "to rule."
   C. "to perceive."
   D. "to teach."

3. **The purpose of the book of Proverbs is**
   A. to experiment.
   B. to theorize.
   C. to teach.
   D. to argue a point of view.

4. **The word *Ecclesiastes* means**
   A. "the scholar."
   B. "the sage."
   C. "the preacher."
   D. "the student."

5. **Ecclesiastes 1-2 deals with**
   A. Solomon's search and recovery.
   B. Solomon's praise of wisdom.
   C. Solomon's song of love.
   D. Solomon's advice to the wealthy.

6. **The term "under the sun" is a**
   A. negative term.
   B. neutral term.
   C. positive term.
   D. undefined term.

7. **The theme of Ecclesiastes is**
   A. vanity of vanities.
   B. eating and drinking.
   C. under the sun.
   D. knowing the true meaning in life through knowing God.

8. **Many ancient interpreters held to the allegorical interpretation of Song of Solomon because**
    A. they knew no other possible view.
    B. they were embarrassed by the sexual descriptions.
    C. Solomon revealed this to be his method.
    D. all the other songs of Solomon were allegorical.

9. **Most modern conservative scholarship interprets the Song of Solomon as**
    A. typical.   C. literal.
    B. allegorical.   D. fictional.

10. **The Song of Solomon is an exposition of**
    A. erotic love in marriage.
    B. spiritual love in marriage.
    C. carnal love in marriage.
    D. genuine love in marriage (Gen. 2:24-25).

What Do You Say?

Have you ever used the concepts found in Proverbs? Please elaborate.

LESSON 5

Pre-Exilic Prophets (Part 1): Obadiah, Joel, Jonah

Prophets of Judgment and Grace

Introduction to the Prophets

The word *prophet* simply means a mouthpiece or spokesman. He was someone who spoke with authority for another. The book of Exodus contains a clear illustration of this meaning where God commissioned Aaron to be Moses' prophet (mouthpiece). When these two men went in before Pharaoh, Aaron would do all the talking; what he spoke was only what Moses instructed him to say. Aaron was not the source of the message, only the mouthpiece to convey the message. Other closely related terms are: *seer* (1 Sam. 9:9), *man of God* (1 Sam. 9:6), *servant of the Lord* (1 Kings 14:18), and *messenger of the Lord* (Hag. 1:13). In a general sense, God calls all believers to be His spokesmen to carry the Gospel to the ends of the earth.

> **Prophets had a preaching ministry of calling upon God's people to obey God's law.**

The prophets were men of consecration, conviction, compassion, and availability. They were not monks or mystics who isolated themselves from the mainstream of life. Some ministered to kings (like Isaiah and Daniel), but most to the common people (like Amos and Ezekiel). Just as the priests represented humanity to God, the prophets represented God to humanity. They were *foretellers* and *forth tellers*. That is, they predicted the future (near and far), and they had a preaching ministry of calling upon God's people to obey God's law.

These men of God who received their messages through dreams, visions, and the audible voice of God used a variety of ways by which to pass on God's message. At times they used just straightforward preaching. Sometimes they used parables and allegories (e.g. Ezek. 15-16). At other times it was through dramatic acting (e.g. Zech. 11). Several times it was through symbolic actions (e.g. 1 Sam. 15:27-31; 1 Kings 11:26-32).

God directed the method of communication; the prophet did not decide for himself (see Hebrews 1:1, "many ways"). God called some of these men to do things which are not necessarily examples for us to follow. We should follow their godly example but not try to imitate their gift and methods of ministry.

The Period of the Prophets

The period of the prophets begins in 1 Samuel 9 and continues through the rest of the history of the Old Testament. In other words, it begins from the start of the reign of Saul, through the era when Israel was a divided kingdom, through the decades when Assyria and Babylonia held the nation captive, including the nation's promised return to the land of

Chart Placing the Prophets by Centuries

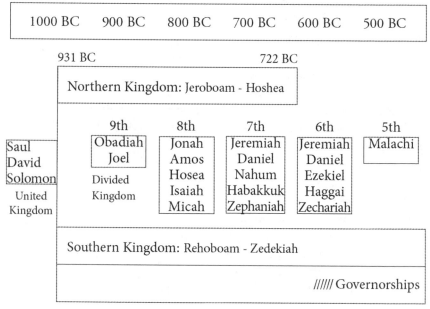

1000 BC	900 BC	800 BC	700 BC	600 BC	500 BC

931 BC   722 BC

Northern Kingdom: Jeroboam - Hoshea

	9th	8th	7th	6th	5th
Saul	Obadiah	Jonah	Jeremiah	Jeremiah	Malachi
David	Joel	Amos	Daniel	Daniel	
Solomon		Hosea	Nahum	Ezekiel	
United	Divided	Isaiah	Habakkuk	Haggai	
Kingdom	Kingdom	Micah	Zephaniah	Zechariah	

Southern Kingdom: Rehoboam - Zedekiah

////// Governorships

Israel. There were many, many prophets during this period. Only a few left us with a written record of their prophecies (Isaiah through Malachi). These "writing prophets" ministered after the division of the kingdom of Israel in 931 BC (see chart). The kingdom was united under Saul, David, and Solomon, but divided into two parts during the reign of Solomon's son, Rehoboam. We find this account in 1 Kings 12 and following. Thus the northern kingdom became very idolatrous, and the southern kingdom continued the line of David.

List of kings and governors of the nation of Israel

	Northern kings (Israel)	Southern kings (Judah)
10th Century	Jeroboam I ..... 931–910 Nadab .... 910–909 Baasha 909–886	Rehoboam ...... 931-913 Abijam .... 913–911 Asa 911–870
9th Century	Mori .... 886–874 Ahab .... 874–853 Ahaziah .... 853–852 Joram .... 852–841 Jehu .... 841–814 Jehoahaz 814–798	Jehoshaphat .. 873–848 Jehoram .... 853–841 Ahaziah .... 841 Athaliah 841–835
8th Century	Jehoash .... 798–782 Jeroboam II ... 793–753 Zechariah ...... 753–752 Shallum .... 752 Pekah .... 752–732 Menahem ...... 752–742 Pekahiah .... 742–740 Hoshea 732–722*	Amaziah .... 796–767 Uzziah .... 790–739 Jotham .... 750–731 Ahaz .... 735–715 Hezekiah 715–686
7th Century		Manasseh ...... 695–642 Amon .... 642–640 Josiah .... 640–609 Jehoahaz .... 609 Jehoiakim 609–597
6th Century		Jehoiachin .... 597 Zedekiah .... 597–586 EXILE Zerubbabel (governor).......... 538-???

5th Century	Ezra (governor) .... 458–??? Nehemiah (governor) .... 445–???

*Note that in the dating of the kings there is some overlap. This is due to the fact that some of the kings reigned at the same time (father and son). We call this *co-regencies*.

Persian kings of the 6th and 5th centuries (539–404 BC)

1.	Cyrus	539–530
2.	Cambyses	530–522
3.	Darius I	522–486
4.	Xerxes	486–464
5.	Artaxerxes I	464–423
6.	Darius II	423–404

Some of the prophets prophesied in the northern kingdom (Israel). They sought to call the people back to the worship of the one true God while condemning their evils and warning of coming judgment. Others prophesied in the southern kingdom (Judah) with a similar message. The northern kingdom lasted from 931–722 BC. God used the Assyrians, as the prophets foretold, to destroy the northern kingdom and to send its people into captivity. The southern kingdom lasted from 931–586 BC until the Babylonians destroyed it, taking away many people.

The time chart shows in which centuries these men of God prophesied. We will follow this order in surveying the prophets. But how do we determine in which century a prophet lived? The chief way is to note what kings were reigning when the prophet prophesied. The superscription (the first verse of a prophetic book, see Hosea 1:1 for example) sometimes gives us this. The historical books of Kings and Chronicles may also mention the prophet (e.g. Jonah in 2 Kings 14:25). Lastly, there may be some historical event within the prophet's book which makes it possible to identify the century (e.g. Nahum 3:8-10).

OBADIAH (NINTH CENTURY BC)

First impressions can be deceiving. One may think that Obadiah is not important because it is the shortest prophetic Old Testament book. Actually, this tiny book packs a powerful message of both judgment and grace. "Great things often come in small packages," as the saying goes.

The Name of the Prophet—Obadiah

Obadiah means *servant of Jehovah (Yahweh)*. About a dozen different men had this name in the Old Testament, but it is impossible to link this prophet with any of them. Our lack of knowledge does not alter our understanding and appreciation of his prophecy, however.

Theme

The theme of Obadiah is the doom of Edom (1:1-16) and the blessing of Israel (1:17-21). Edom descended from Esau (Gen. 36), who was Jacob's twin brother (Gen. 25:19-26). Just as Esau and Jacob were enemies, so were their descendants until God destroyed Edom.

Location of Edom

Edom lay south of the Dead Sea. God had appointed Edom (Esau) its land portion as found in Genesis 27:39. The region was known as Mt. Seir, a very rugged and mountainous area. In it was a rock fortress called Sela (Petra), the capital city of ancient Edom. The Edomites in their arrogant self-confidence believed that no one could destroy them (Obad. 3-4). God could and did!

Summary of the Book

The prophecy is quite easy to follow. Edom is despised and God will make it small among the nations. Its rock fortress will not be a safe refuge from God, and it will be completely ravaged. Ironically, Edom's allies will turn against it, and its wisdom and military power will be destroyed. Edom is simply reaping what it has sown, and God is just in judging it. What Edom experiences will be what all nations experience in the "day of the LORD" (1:1-17). In contrast, God will greatly bless Israel. He will deliver it from oppression, triumph over its enemies, restore its land, and reign over it (1:17-21). God is going to have the last word in the history of man. Jesus shall reign! Is He king of your life now?

Principle of Judgment

The principle of judgment by which God will judge Edom and all the nations is stated in verse 15: "As you have done, it shall be done to you; your deeds shall return on your own head." This is retributive justice. That is, Edom will reap what it has sown. Has Edom cut off Israel? Then Edom will be cut off. Has Edom ransacked Jerusalem? So Edom's rock fortress will be ransacked. Has Edom slaughtered Israel? So Edom will be slain.

Edom followed its fleshly desires and paid for it. We too will reap what we have sown (Gal. 6:7-8). It is an unchanging divine law. Let us be careful to allow the Holy Spirit to control us. Let us invest our lives in spiritual and eternal things. Edom's arrogance was its undoing. Let us humble ourselves under God's almighty hand!

JOEL (NINTH CENTURY BC)

In Proverbs 3:11-12 we read that one way in which God shows His love to His people is to afflict them with the rod of chastening, or discipline—to cause them pain. That was what God was doing in Joel. Sometimes God can get our attention only by allowing suffering to come into our lives. The Israel of Joel's day had sinned greatly against God and had not repented. In response, God had brought down a locust plague upon the nation (1:1–2:11). Not all suffering is the result of personal or national sin, but in this case it is, as seen by Joel's call to repentance (2:12-17).

The Name of the Prophet—Joel

The name means *Jehovah (Yahweh) is God.* When Joel's parents named him they were confessing their loyalty to the true God. What is our confession? Is it *Jesus is Lord?* If so, then may our lives match this testimony of our lips.

The Theme

Have you noticed an important recurring expression as you read Joel? It is "the day of the Lord." Several times this term is used (1:15; 2:1, 11, 31; 3:14). Other prophets used it, too. The theme of the book of Joel is the day of the Lord. What does this mean? The term is used primarily in the Old Testament of God's judgment (Isa. 2:12; 10:20; 13:6, 9; Ezek. 13:5; 30:3; Amos 5:18-20: Zeph. 1:7-15; Zech. 14:1, and many more). It is not necessarily just a twenty-four-hour day but rather a specific period of time. The Old Testament uses "the day of the Lord" to refer to judgments which God brought on His people in ancient days. It is also used of a still future day of judgment in the end times.

Joel used the term in both ways: The first section (1:1–2:27) is about the time of Joel when God brought His judgment upon the southern kingdom in the form of a locust invasion. The second section (2:28–3:21) is about a future day of the Lord when mighty judgments will destroy the earth. In that day when God will judge His enemies, He will also save His people and bless them with the Holy Spirit (2:28-29). All this will culminate in establishing God's kingdom upon the earth (3:18-21).

Summary of the Book

Locusts had devastated the land of Israel by devouring everything in their path (1:4). A locust invasion of billions of the small creatures was one of the judgments predicted by Moses (Deut. 28) which God would use when His people sinned. Many scholars believe Judah's sin was the worship of Baal—one of the pagan deities of the ancient Canaanites. They further identify the time of the locust invasion as during the reign of the wicked Baal worshiper, Queen Athaliah (2 Kings 11; 2 Chron. 23-24). She was the daughter of Jezebel in the northern kingdom. Joel called upon the nation to mourn and lament "for the day of the Lord is near" (1:15). He compared the severity of the locust invasion to a human army (2:1-11).Then he called upon the nation to repent (2:12-17). He promised that the Lord would then remove the locusts and restore the devastated land (2:18-27).

Leaping over the centuries to a time still future to us, Joel prophesied of a time in which God's judgment will engulf the whole earth (see Revelation 6-19). At that time (1) God will intervene on behalf of His people Israel (2:32) to save from destruction "everyone who calls on the name of the

LORD;" (2) He will judge all the surrounding nations (3:9-17); (3) and He will bring in the kingdom so often promised in the Prophets (3:18-21).

The Promise of the Spirit

When the apostle Peter preached his sermon at Pentecost, he quoted from Joel 2:28-29 (Acts 2:17-18). Peter did not say that these verses were fulfilled on the day of Pentecost, when the Holy Spirit descended upon the church. Actually, these verses will not be fulfilled until after the church is raptured to heaven. The Holy Spirit's coming on Pentecost was simply an illustration of what will happen in the future. The future converted nation of Israel will have the fullness of the Holy Spirit as prophesied by Joel.

God has graced the church in this era with the indwelling, baptism, and filling of the Holy Spirit so that we might fulfill our calling.

JONAH (EIGHTH CENTURY BC)

Jonah is probably the best known of the minor prophets. Why? Because it is a story about the man rather than a record of his prophecies. It is easy to remember stories about famous people who have done great exploits. God wants us to learn about this man because in doing so we will learn a great deal about ourselves!

His Name—Jonah

Jonah's name means *dove*. The dove is a symbol of peace. Someone has commented that Jonah was more like a hawk than a dove because he didn't want God to spare ancient Nineveh from the judgment he had preached. God wanted Jonah to be a messenger of peace to the wicked sinners of Nineveh, but peace could only come as they heard a message of judgment: "Yet forty days, and Nineveh shall be overthrown!"

His Background

Unlike Obadiah and Joel, we know at least five things about Jonah's background. (1) His father's name is Amittai (Jonah 1:1; 2 Kings 14:25); (2) Jonah prophesied during the reign of Jeroboam II (see the charts) who reigned in the northern kingdom from 793–753 BC Jonah prophesied some military success for this wicked king (2 Kings 14:25); (3) we learn that he was from the town of Gath-hepher. This was a town in the tribal area of Zebulon, and it was near the Sea of Galilee (2 Kings 14:25). Gath-hepher was about three miles from Nazareth, where several centuries later Jesus grew up into manhood. Other prophets ministered in Northern Palestine (Hosea, Amos), but the greatest of them all was Jesus who said in Matthew 12:41: "[One] greater than Jonah is here;" (4) we learn in comparing Jonah 1:17 with Matthew 12:40 that Jonah was a type of our Lord Jesus Christ in His burial and resurrection: "For just as Jonah was three days and three nights in the belly of the great fish, so will the Son of Man be three days and three nights in the heart of the earth;" (5) we learn in comparing Jonah 3 with Luke 11:29-30 that Jonah himself was a sign to the Ninevites. Evidently, they knew of his experience in the great fish, and this reinforced his message of judgment.

The Theme of Jonah

The theme of Jonah is Jonah's relation to the will of God in his service as a prophet. God is very interested in the maturing and development of His servants. He knows that when we first come to Christ and begin to serve Him, there are rough edges which need to be smoothed and polished so we can more acceptably serve Him more acceptably. But Jonah was no newcomer; he was already an active prophet (2 Kings 14:23-25). Even mature servants, however, need to grow and develop. There is always room for improvement, and Jonah was no exception. Jonah is a classic example of a servant of God who put his will above the will of God. He thought that he knew better than God, at least at this particular time in his life.

Summary of the Book

In chapter 1 Jonah is presumptuous, disobeying God's command to go to Nineveh and preach against it. In chapter 2, because of God's dealing with him, Jonah vowed desperately to turn back to doing God's will. In chapter 3, Jonah obeyed instantly. Chapter 4, however, demonstrates that obedience is not always a guarantee of a right spirit or attitude. Jonah, the most successful evangelist-prophet of the Old Testament, was displeased with the outcome! He was angry over the conversion of an entire city! Jonah was in desperate need of correction, and our loving Lord was going to see that he got it. God loved Jonah too much to let him get away with his unfounded anger. He corrected him (4:5-11) by means of the plant and the east wind to see the unreasonableness of his anger. The plant that Jonah cared so much about came up in one night and then disappeared, but the souls of the Ninevites were eternal.

Jonah must have profited by this correction since he afterwards wrote this story. Have you profited by it? Do you have an impartial love for all mankind? Do you love your neighbor?

LESSON 5 EXAM

Use the exam sheet that has been provided to complete your exam.

1. **The word *prophet* simply means**
   A. "holy man."   C. "intercessor."
   B. "spokesman."   D. "preacher."

2. **The period of the Prophets was from**
   A. Deuteronomy to Judges.
   B. 1 Samuel 9 through Malachi.
   C. 1 Kings through 2 Kings.
   D. 1 Kings through Nehemiah.

3. **The writing prophets ministered**
   A. from the 11th to the 7th centuries BC.
   B. from the 10th to the 6th centuries BC.
   C. from the 9th to the 5th centuries BC.
   D. from the 8th to the 4th centuries BC.

4. **The nation of Edom was located**
   A. south of the Dead Sea.
   B. north of the Sea of Galilee.
   C. west of Jerusalem.
   D. east of Bethel.

5. **Judah and Jerusalem were suffering in Joel's time because of**
   A. earthquake and floods.
   B. invasion of a foreign army.
   C. disease and famine.
   D. a locust plague.

6. **The theme of Joel is**
   A. the King and the kingdom.
   B. the just shall live by faith.
   C. the day of the Lord.
   D. consolation and comfort.

7. **Joel's name means**
   A. "strength of Jehovah."
   B. "salvation of Jehovah."
   C. "Jehovah is God."
   D. "Jehovah is righteous."

8. **Jonah is a type of our Lord Jesus Christ**
   A. in his birth.
   B. in his life.
   C. in his death.
   D. in his burial and resurrection.

9. **The theme of Jonah is**
   A. God's love for all mankind.
   B. God's correction of Jonah for his attitude.
   C. Jonah himself in relation to the will of God regarding his service.
   D. the prejudice of Israel against the Assyrians.

10. **Jonah's name means**
    A. "hawk."   C. "lamb."
    B. "dove."   D. "ram."

What Do You Say?

How important is one's attitude when it comes to serving God (compare Jonah 4)?

_____

_____

_____

_____

Pre-Exilic Prophets (Part 2): Amos Hosea, Micah

AMOS (EIGHTH CENTURY BC)

D o you respect a man with courage? Do you admire a man who not only has well-founded convictions but who also stands up for what he believes, no matter the cost? Do you love a man who has a keen sense of justice but who is willing in the face of stern opposition to stand up for the rights and needs of the powerless and poor? If your answer is "yes," then Amos is your man!

Amos was all these things as a servant of the Lord. He was a dynamic person who ministered in a day when society, religion, and government were bankrupt. He delivered a convicting, perturbing indictment against Israel (the northern kingdom). He was strongly opposed (7:10-17), but he never gave up. Still today we need men and women who have the strength Amos had to challenge the sin in our society!

The Name of the Prophet—Amos

Amos means *burden-bearer,* and it fits the prophetic responsibility God gave him. He bore the burden of divine judgment against Israel, Judah and the pagan nations. But he especially targeted the northern kingdom.

The Location of the Prophet—Tekoa

Not all the prophets were from a big city. Some, like Isaiah, were born and brought up in Jerusalem were the temple and palace were. Others, like Amos, grew up in relative obscurity. Tekoa was about 12 miles south of Jerusalem. It was a wild and desolate place—a very rugged area. The personality of Amos was somewhat like the land in which he grew up. This was just the kind of man God needed to preach His work of judgment at Bethel.

The Occupation of Amos

Some people need to hold two jobs to support themselves. A resident of Tekoa like Amos had a hard time doing that. He was a "herdsman and a dresser of sycamore figs" (Amos 7:14b). Cultivating the fruit of the sycamore tree was among the lowest jobs in Palestine. It was a seasonal occupation. Several times a year, Amos traveled to the coastal plain or the Jordan Valley where the trees were farmed. Amos' migrant work took him into the northern kingdom. Little did he realize that one day he would go there not to "pick fruit" but to "bear fruit" for God by preaching God's message of judgment at Bethel. It may be that God will call *you* from secular work to full-time service one day. Be ready!

The Theme of Amos

It only takes one reading of the book to discover that its theme is the judgment of God. God is a just God. When His holy laws are violated, He impartially judges those who will not repent. Several nations surrounding Palestine, as well as Judah and Israel, were threatened with His judgment. But it is sinful Israel that is primarily in view in the book. The judgment messages delivered by Amos at Bethel were "contingency prophecies." That is, if Israel would repent, then God would not judge them. God had already been chastising the northern kingdom (4:6-11). Now He threatened its destruction and the exile of its people (3:11-15; 4:2, 3; 4:12-13; 5:1-3, 11, 16-27; 6:7-14; 7:7-9; 8:1-3; 9:1-10). We know that Israel did not repent. God fulfilled these prophecies by using the cruel Assyrian nation to carry them away into exile (2 Kings 15-17). The nation that forgets God and goes its own way will reap what it has sown.

Summary of the Book

The first two chapters consist of eight prophetic burdens of judgment. Amos lashes out at six neighboring nations of Palestine. Then he turns the spotlight of condemnation upon Judah and Israel (2:4-6). This teaches us that God is no respecter of persons. Judah and Israel came under greater judgment because they sinned knowing God much more intimately.

Chapters 3–6 are made up of three sermons of judgment. From the general messages of judgment in chapters 1–2, Amos now addresses the Northern Kingdom. These sermons have many similarities:

- They each have the same beginning—"hear this word."
- They each contain severe rebukes for sin.
- They each speak of the judgment God will bring if there is no repentance.
- They each have some element which should have motivated Israel to turn back to God (like the fact that they are the chosen people; 3:2).
- They each contain some pathetic expression of the awful spiritual condition of the northern kingdom.

See if you can pick out some of these similarities.

Amos 7:1-9:10 consists of five prophetic visions. Amos not only hears the communication of God's word, but he also sees it. These visions progressively convey the various aspects of judgment.

1. Vision of devouring locusts; judgment averted (7:1-6)
2. Vision of the plumb line; judgment determined (7:7-9)
3. Historical interlude; Amos opposed (7:10-17)
4. Vision of summer fruit; judgment inevitable (8:1-14)
5. Vision of the altar; judgment inescapable (9:1-10)

Amos 9:11-15 is the only bright part of the prophecy. Like Obadiah and Joel, Amos ends his prophecy positively with the future restoration of Israel. There will be the restoration of the Davidic dynasty (9:11a) in the nation (9:11b-12), abundant agriculture (9:13), the people (9:14a), liberty (9:14b), and their permanency in Israel (9:15).

In summary, Amos gave the bad news (1:1-9:10) before he could give the good news (9:11-15). It is never easy to confront God's people with judgment. But it is always delightful to hold out hope to sinners who recognize their need for God. Let God use you to do this.

HOSEA (EIGHTH CENTURY BC)

The prophets were sometimes called upon to bear great grief and suffering during their ministries. Ezekiel, Jeremiah, and Hosea experienced suffering in one particular area. How would you like it if the Lord spoke to you one day and said, "I am going to take your beloved wife from you in death"? That is what happened to Ezekiel (24:16). How would you respond if the Lord said to you, "Young man, or young woman, I am not going to let you get married. You must remain single in service." That happened to Jeremiah (16:1-4). How would you feel if you married a person you deeply loved and he or she became unfaithful? That was Hosea's experience! The Bible makes it clear that the experience of each of these godly men was a "sign" to the nation of Israel.

The Name of the Prophet—Hosea

Hosea's name means *salvation*. God had been offering salvation to Israel through Amos and now through Hosea. They offered not only a salvation from sin, but also freedom from the domination of foreign powers. All Israel had to do was turn to the Lord in sincerity and repentance, and salvation would be theirs. Is salvation what you need? You can have it in Jesus Christ. You can be saved from God's wrath through Him (Rom. 5:9).

The Location of the Prophet

We know very little about where Hosea lived. We know he prophesied primarily against the northern kingdom. In Hosea 7:5 he speaks of "our king" which is Jeroboam II, king of the northern kingdom, possibly at Bethel or Samaria. But wherever he lived, this sensitive man was greatly burdened as he observed Israel's daily apostasy. He could not get used to sin. Neither should we!

The Theme of Hosea

Hosea's theme is love—the unfailing love of God to Israel. God's love is unfailing to His people because it is unconditional in nature. God loves His people, not for anything in themselves, but because it is His nature to love. In the book of Hosea, God's unfailing love is dramatized in the marriage of Hosea and his wife Gomer (chapters 1–3). It is expounded in Hosea's sermons (chapters 4–14) which emphasize the relationship between God and Israel. The unfailing love of God for Israel is the kind of love He has for us through Jesus Christ. It is a love that can never be bought or destroyed.

Summary of the Book

1. The Unfailing Love of God to Israel is Illustrated and Dramatized in the Life of Hosea and His Family (1–3)

- The *marriage and family* of Hosea are symbolic of God's relationship to the nation of Israel (1:1–2:1).
- The *separation* of Hosea from Gomer is symbolic of God's chastisement of Israel for her unfaithfulness (2:2-23).
- The *restoration* of Gomer to Hosea is symbolic of Israel's restoration to Jehovah (Yahweh) in a coming day (3).

2. The Unfailing Love of God to Israel is Expounded by Hosea in Sermon Form (4–14)

- God's unfailing love to Israel cannot cover her sin, for *God is holy* and sin must be exposed (4–8).
- God's unfailing love to Israel cannot pass by her sin, for *God is just* and sin must be punished (9–11).
- God's unfailing love for Israel will not give her up to total destruction for *He is faithful* to His promises (11–14).

A Major Problem in Hosea

Did God really command Hosea to marry a prostitute (1:2)? Was she one before he married her, or did she become one after they married? We should take this story literally, but there are those who differ in their opinions. Some hold that she was a prostitute at the time of the marriage. They believe that the holy God commanded Hosea to do something contradicting His holiness. Others teach that Gomer was a chaste woman when she married Hosea and that she later became unfaithful. This is the most suitable explanation of the literal view for two reasons. First, this view is clear from chapter 3. There, Hosea takes Gomer back to himself after having rejected her before for adultery. This rejection is not justifiable if Hosea had knowingly married a prostitute. Second, this view fits perfectly with the analogy which the Holy Spirit gives between Jehovah and Israel: "Go, take to yourself a wife of whoredom and have children of whoredom, for the land commits great whoredom by forsaking the LORD" (1:2). The word "land" refers to the nation. If the nation has departed from the Lord, it seems that the nation was once in fellowship with Him. Israel was a chaste bride when Jehovah "married" her at Mt. Sinai when God made His covenant with Israel (Exodus 19). Jeremiah 2:1-3 speaks of Israel's chastity which was later lost through idolatry and foreign alliances.

MICAH (EIGHTH CENTURY BC)

What do you think of first when the prophet Micah comes to mind? That's right, the birthplace of Jesus (compare Mic. 5:2 with Matt. 2:5-6). Micah was the only prophet to reveal the place of His birth—Bethlehem in Judah. Unfortunately, this is the only thing that many believers know about this fascinating book. May this lesson stimulate your interest to study this great prophet in detail.

The Name of the Prophet—Micah

Some people hate their name so much that they have it legally changed. Anyone in Israel with the name Micah (and there were seven mentioned in the Old Testament) would have been proud to bear that name, for it means *Who is like Jehovah?* Micah is a short version of Micaiah (just as Jim is for James). There is a play on this name in 7:18: "Who is a God like you, pardoning iniquity ..." Israel needs pardon and God is ready to extend it to them if they repent.

The Location of the Prophet

Micah was from the village of Moresheth. It was situated twenty miles southwest of Jerusalem and was very near Gath in Philistia. It was not far from the famous city of Lachish, close to the highway from Mesopotamia to Egypt.

Though Micah was from Moresheth, he evidently did his prophesying in Jerusalem. His story is a case of a small-town boy coming to the big city. In Jerusalem he preached against the two kingdoms in general and specifically against the wealthy land-grabbers, leaders, prophets, and priests. Jeremiah mentions Micah's ministry to Hezekiah and the people during Hezekiah's reign (Jer. 26:16-19).

The Theme of Micah

Micah's theme is the judgment and kingdom of God. Some of the predictions of judgment have been fulfilled (1:5-6), but some are still future (5:10-15). The kingdom predictions, except the announcement of Christ's birthplace, are still to be fulfilled. Micah and Isaiah were contemporaries, and some of Micah's prophecies echo in Isaiah (compare Mic. 4:1-3 with Isa. 2:1-4).

The International Setting of His Ministry

The Syrian empire, which God had used against the northern kingdom, was now weak and about to fall. The Assyrian empire was the power to be reckoned with. The Assyrians would destroy Syria in 732 BC, and ten years later Israel would fall to this mighty power. God not only uses nature (Joel 1-2), but He also uses nations to correct and punish His erring children. The northern kingdom was on the brink of disaster. The southern kingdom to which Micah ministered was politically, morally, and spiritually sick (see Isaiah 1).

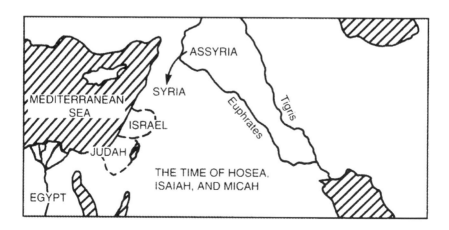

Summary of the Book

The first major section (chapters 1–3) announces judgment on the divided kingdom generally (chapter 1). It then denounces men of wealth and position in particular (chapters 2–3).

The second major section (chapters 4–5) contrasts the future King and kingdom of God with past judgment. The kingdom of the past failed and ultimately was destroyed through invasions and captivities. But God consistently held out the promise of a glorious kingdom ruled by His beloved Son, Jesus Christ. In this section, the future kingdom is contrasted with the past. There are many abrupt changes throughout this section. It switches back and forth between the past and the future.

The last section (chapters 6–7) deals primarily with judgment but in a different form from the first two. It is in the form of a court case. Jehovah is judge, Micah is the prosecuting attorney, creation is both witness and jury, and Israel is the defendant. The Judge has a complaint against His people. They are guilty, but there is hope.

The prophecy of Micah begins with a picture of the Lord coming to judge and ends with Him coming to bless. Three excellencies of the Lord are presented: His forgiving love (7:18), His redeeming power (7:19), and His unfailing faithfulness (7:20). Hope shines even in the darkest hour.

LESSON 6 EXAM

Use the exam sheet that has been provided to complete your exam.

1. **Amos was from the city of**
   A. Bethlehem.
   B. Jerusalem.
   C. Hebron.
   D. Tekoa.

2. **The theme of Amos is**
   A. the judgment of God.
   B. the triumph of grace.
   C. mercy to the Gentiles.
   D. God's enduring love.

3. **Hosea suffered in the domestic area of life just like**
   A. Obadiah and Amos.
   B. Zechariah and Malachi.
   C. Nahum and Habakkuk.
   D. Ezekiel and Jeremiah.

4. **The theme of Hosea is**
   A. the unfailing love of God to Israel.
   B. the justice and wrath of God.
   C. the redemption of the Gentiles.
   D. the coming Antichrist.

5. **Hosea 4-14 views God as**
   A. holy, just and faithful.
   B. omnipotent, immutable, and gracious.
   C. benevolent, longsuffering and patient.
   D. wise, omnipresent, merciful.

6. **A major problem in Hosea concerns the**
   A. truthfulness of the book.
   B. time element of the book.
   C. command of God for Hosea to marry a prostitute.
   D. place where Hosea lived.

7. **Hosea's name means**
   A. "praise."
   B. "salvation."
   C. "remembrance."
   D. "righteousness."

8. **Micah's name means**
   A. "precious of the Lord"
   B. "power of the Lord"
   C. "who is like Jehovah?"
   D. "who will speak for Jehovah?"

9. **The theme of Micah is**
   A. the judgment and kingdom of God.
   B. the King and kingdom of God.
   C. the fall of Jerusalem.
   D. the birthplace of Jesus.

10. **Micah was a contemporary of**
   A. Obadiah.
   B. Habakkuk.
   C. Nahum.
   D. Isaiah.

What Do You Say?

Do you think you could love your fellow believers unconditionally and unfailingly as Hosea did his wife? Why? How?

_____

_____

_____

_____

Pre-Exilic Prophets (Part 3): Isaiah

The Prophet of Judgment and Consolation

As a prophet, Isaiah was in a class by himself. Scholars praise him as having no peer among the prophets, as being the prince of the prophets, and as being the greatest among the writing prophets. What do the scholars mean? First, they are referring to his great literary skills (vocabulary, diction, style, poetic imagery). Second, they are referring to his ability to organize his message and communicate it effectively. His book is beautifully arranged and shows the unity, coherence, and emphasis of a great work. Third, they are referring to his being inspired by God to write the most comprehensive prophetic book in the Old Testament.

Isaiah has been rightfully called the Old Testament evangelistic prophet.

One example is the massive coverage he gives to the coming Messianic King and kingdom. Isaiah has been rightfully called the Old Testament evangelistic prophet in that he published the good news of the Gospel seven hundred years before Jesus' first advent. The best known passage in Isaiah predicting the Lord's sufferings is the familiar fifty-third chapter. The New Testament quotes this chapter several times to prove that the Messiah needed to suffer before entering into His glory.

Isaiah was not the most outstanding Old Testament prophet in the realm of personal godliness, however. Jeremiah, for instance, was as holy as Isaiah. We must understand this distinction lest we think of ourselves as second-class citizens in the kingdom of God. God will reward us someday in heaven. It will not be for the gifts and abilities we have, but for what dedicated service we rendered to Him with the gifts He gave us! Be encouraged. God simply requires us to be faithful.

The Author of Isaiah

Chapter 1 makes it clear that this is the "vision of Isaiah the son of Amoz" (1:1). Isaiah's name means *Jehovah is salvation*. The meaning fits the general theme of his book.

We do not know very much about Isaiah's family background. His father's name was Amos (not to be confused with the prophet Amos). He had a wife who possessed the prophetic gift (8:3) and two sons (7:3; 8:1-3).

Isaiah lived in the city of Jerusalem. In fact, he mentions Jerusalem forty-nine times. He was a prophet to Jerusalem and the southern kingdom of Judah (1:1). He had access to the royal court of the kings, directing much of his ministry to the ruling class.

His call to the prophetic ministry is recorded

> **Isaiah's name means "Jehovah (YAHWEH) is salvation."**

in Isaiah 6. It came in the year that good King Uzziah died (739 BC). It was preceded by an awesome vision of "the Lord sitting upon a throne, high and lifted up; and the train of his robe filled the temple" (6:1). The seraphim attended the Lord and they cried out, "Holy, holy, holy is the LORD of hosts; the whole earth is full of his glory" (6:2-3).

This vision of the holiness and glory of God had a sobering effect on Isaiah, for he felt the depth of his sin and he cried out, "Woe is me! For I am lost; for I am a man of unclean lips, and I dwell in the midst of a people of unclean lips; for my eyes have seen the King, the LORD of hosts" (6:4-5). When he confessed his sin, God cleansed him and made him ready for his commission (6:6-7) to preach in Jerusalem and Judah (6:8-13). This teaches us that in order to serve God fruitfully we must admit our sin and humble ourselves before Him for our cleansing. God uses the person who is "humble and contrite in spirit and trembles at [His] word"! (66:2)

The Times of Isaiah (1:1)

Isaiah prophesied during the reigns of Uzziah, Jotham, Ahaz, and Hezekiah, kings of Judah. For background see 2 Kings 14-20 and 2 Chronicles 26-32.

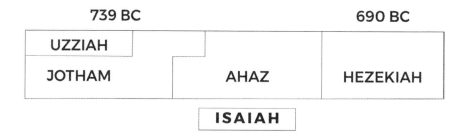

The Reigns of Uzziah and Jotham (2 Kings 14:15; 2 Chron. 26-27)

The long reign of Uzziah was marked by great prosperity in Judah. With prosperity came the general corruption of the spiritual, moral, and religious life of Judah. These conditions of decay continued into the reign of Jotham.

The Reign of Ahaz (2 Kings 16; 2 Chron. 28)

King Ahaz was one of the worst kings ever to reign in Judah. He was fearful, cowardly, and unbelieving. He introduced into the southern kingdom polluting idolatries of all kinds. During his reign, Judah was threatened by a coalition of the northern kingdom and Syria. Isaiah confronted Ahaz to trust the Lord and not give way to fear (chapter 7). Instead, Ahaz followed his own cowardly heart and aligned himself with the wicked Assyrian nation. This was the beginning of very serious trouble for Judah for years to come.

The Reign of Hezekiah (2 Kings 18-20; 2 Chron. 29-32)

Hezekiah had a heart for God! He was one of the few religious reformers in the southern kingdom. Both Isaiah and 2 Kings suggest that Isaiah assisted Hezekiah in his reforms. Two significant events took place during Hezekiah's reign: (1) The fall of the northern kingdom in 722 BC at the hands of the Assyrians, and (2) the supernatural destruction of the Assyrian army under Sennacherib in 701 BC.

2 Chronicles 29-31 records the reforms of Hezekiah in great detail. It must have been thrilling to the prophet Isaiah to see his good friend Hezekiah take such a resolute stand against evil in the nation. Hezekiah's

trust in the Lord led to bold moral and religious ventures (2 Kings 18:3-6). We may never have the position and power of Hezekiah, but we can have the heart for God that he manifested. Trust Him (Prov. 3:5-6)!

The Structure of the Book of Isaiah

1. Prophecies of Judgment (1–35)

- Against Judah and Jerusalem (1–12)
- Against surrounding Nations (13–23)
- Against the whole world (24–35)

2. Historical Transition (36–39)

- Destruction of Judah averted (36–37)
- Death of King Hezekiah averted (38–39)

3. Prophecies of Hope and Comfort (40–66)

- Of restoration to the land (40–48)
- Of salvation of the soul (49–57)
- Of second coming and kingdom (58–66)

Some Observations Concerning the First Section (1–35)

- Though the heading speaks of judgment, there are a few chapters (2, 11, 12, and others) that point to future glory and blessing for Israel and the world.
- Chapter 1 is the keynote chapter for the first section. It is a scathing denunciation of Israel for its incredible sins. Isaiah calls for repentance and change (1:16-18), for there is still hope.
- Assyria is the great world power during this time, and it is this nation which God threatens to use in judgment against His rebellious people. God calls Assyria "the rod of my anger; the staff in their hands is my fury" (10:5). However, God will judge Assyria for its arrogance and self-sufficiency (10:5-12; book of Nahum).
- The great majority of the prophecies in this section have been fulfilled.

Some Observations about the Central Section (36–39)

- These chapters consist of two distinct sections. The first section (chapters 36–37) describes the Assyrian invasion of Judah and Jerusalem in 701 BC. At this time God miraculously saved Jerusalem from the Assyrians by killing 185,000 of them. Godly King Hezekiah was reigning and Isaiah ministered to him. The second section tells how God preserved Hezekiah from death and added more years to his life. It also describes how Hezekiah received the Babylonian delegation who came to visit him upon hearing that he had been healed. Hezekiah proudly showed to the Babylonians all his treasures. Isaiah prophesied that they would one day invade Judah and carry all of it away!
- These chapters form a bridge from the first major section (chapters 1–35) to the second (chapters 40–66). Chapters 36–37 conclude the first section by showing God's judgment upon the Assyrians. Chapters 38–39 form an introduction to the second major section. They introduce the future great enemy from whom Israel will be delivered by King Cyrus of the Persians (chapters 40–49).

Some Observations Concerning the Third Section (40–66)

- The heading speaks of hope and comfort, but there are some chapters (like 41 and 47) that deal with judgment against the foes of God's people Israel.
- This major section divides evenly into three sections of nine chapters each (40–48; 49–57; 58–66). At the end of each section there is a negative statement about the wicked (48:22; 57:20-21; 66:24). The student should take time to read these. The first two are similar, declaring that there is no peace for the wicked. The last speaks of terrible torment.
- Chapter 40 is the keynote chapter for this major division. This chapter begins the emphasis on hope and comfort (40:1-11). Then it describes the awesome power and person of God who will bring the comfort (40:12-31).
- Chapters 40–48 primarily deal with the future deliverance of Israel from the Babylonian exile. God will use Cyrus to defeat the

Babylonians and allow the Jewish people to return to Israel. Cyrus is a type of Jesus Christ, who will bring an even greater deliverance to His people—salvation from sin, death, and hell. It is interesting that Cyrus was mentioned by Isaiah (44:28; 45:1) many, many years before he was born. Isaiah prophesied in the eighth century and Cyrus appeared in the sixth. He destroyed the Babylonian Empire, and Persia took over the Middle East (539 BC). Ezra recorded the proclamation of Cyrus that allowed the Jewish exiles to return to Israel (Ezra 1:1-4).

- Chapters 49–57 form an outstanding section concerning the coming of the Messiah. It predicts the Messiah's mission (chapter 49), His obedience (chapter 50), His encouragement to the righteous (51:1–52:12). His death on the cross (52:13–53:12), His universal blessing to Israel and the nations (54:1–56:8), and His condemnation of the wicked in Israel (56:9–57:21).

- Chapters 58–66 bring the book of Isaiah to a climax. It may be divided into the following four divisions:

1. *58–60:* This section deals with Israel's sin (58:1–59:8), confession (59:9-15), and the second coming of Messiah bringing glory to Israel (chapter 60)

2. *61–62:* This section predicts the ministry of the Messiah at His first (61:1-2a) and second (61:2b-11) coming. It climaxes with a very beautiful picture of God's favor on Jerusalem (chapter 62).

3. *63–65:* This section may be entitled The Great Day of the Lord. It is a day when great vengeance will come upon the earth (63:1-6). Israel will ask for God's intervention in this time of severe judgment (63:7–64:12). The Lord will graciously intervene (chapter 65).

4. *66:* The concluding chapter contrasts the humble and the wicked, judgment and blessing. The nation of Israel will be reborn and experience God's glory. The wicked will suffer eternal torment (66:24). The chapter begins by identifying the person to whom God looks with favor—it is the humble and contrite one who trembles at God's word (66:1-2). May God find us to be that kind of person so that we may experience His blessing.

Messianic Prophecies of Christ's Suffering and Death

There is no other prophet who gives more messianic prophecies than Isaiah. He predicted the virgin birth of Christ (7:14), His humanity (11:1), His deity (9:6; 40:9), His ministry (9:1-2), His death, burial, and resurrection (52:13–53:12), and much more. The passage dealing with Christ's suffering and death is one of the best known of all messianic prophecies. Observe the following outline of this outstanding prophecy.

1. The Supreme Servant of the Lord (52:13-15)

Exalted (52:13), humiliated (52:14), and manifested as an atoning Savior (52:15).

2. The Scorned Servant of the Lord (53:1-3)

He was scorned regarding His message (53:1) and His person (53:2-3).

3. The Suffering Servant of the Lord (53:4-6)

These verses form Israel's main confession concerning the reason for Christ's suffering. The false reason is given in 53:4b, and the true reason (atonement) is given in 53:4a, 5-6.

4. The Submissive Servant of the Lord (53:7-9)

The previous point emphasized *why* He suffered. These verses emphasize *how* He suffered. He was submissive to the will of God.

5. The Successful Servant of the Lord (53:10-12)

Many of God's servants were successful in their work, but no one succeeded like Jesus. The reason for His success is first stated (53:10a), and then the marvelous results are given for Him and for those who believe in Him (53:10b-12).

This passage has been described as the Mt. Everest of biblical prophecy concerning Christ's suffering and death. That is, Isaiah 52:13–53:12 gives us the highest and clearest view of Christ's sufferings in the Old Testament. We should read it often and ask God to make our hearts thankful for what our Lord Jesus has done for us!

LESSON 7 EXAM

Use the exam sheet that has been provided to complete your exam.

1. **Isaiah has been called**
    A. the most intelligent prophet.
    B. the richest prophet.
    C. the evangelistic prophet.
    D. the oldest prophet.

2. **Isaiah's name, which fits the general theme of the book, means**
    A. "Jehovah is salvation."
    B. "Jehovah lifts up."
    C. "Jehovah, my righteousness."
    D. "Jehovah is coming."

3. **Isaiah's vision of the Lord on His throne caused him to feel**
    A. the depth of his sin.
    B. confidence in his prophetic gift.
    C. sorrow for sinful Judah.
    D. insecure about the future.

4. **King Ahaz was noted for being**
    A. an outstanding military leader.
    B. a godly example to Judah.
    C. one of the worst kings to reign over Judah.
    D. courageous and fearless as a leader.

5. **The great world power of the first 35 chapters of Isaiah was**
    A. Syria.   C. Egypt.
    B. Assyria.   D. Babylon.

6. **The first 35 chapters of Isaiah deal mostly with**
    A. God's blessing upon Judah.
    B. God's judgment upon Judah and Jerusalem and the whole world.
    C. the Messiah's kingdom for 1,000 years.
    D. the Messiah's suffering.

7. **The purpose of Isaiah 36-39 is to**
   A. form a bridge from 1-35 to 40-66.
   B. explain the need for Messiah to die.
   C. predict the rise of the Roman empire.
   D. give background on Isaiah's family.

8. **Chapter 40 is the keynote chapter of the last major section of Isaiah, it describes in part**
   A. the awesome power and person of God.
   B. the splendor of God's future kingdom.
   C. the awesomeness of the Day of the Lord.
   D. the suffering of God's Messiah.

9. **The great world leader of chapters 40-48 who is a type of Jesus as deliverer of His people is**
   A. Nebuchadnezzar.   C. Tiglath-pileser.
   B. Darius 1.   D. Cyrus.

10. **There is no prophet who gives more Messianic prophecies than**
    A. Isaiah.   C. Ezekiel.
    B. Jeremiah.   D. Daniel.

What Do You Say?

What is it about Isaiah 53 that affects you the most?

Pre-Exilic prophets (Part 4): Nahum, Zephaniah, Habakkuk

NAHUM (SEVENTH CENTURY BC)

Jonah and Nahum both preached judgment against the ancient city of Nineveh, capital of Assyria. Jonah's words were few: "Yet forty days, and Nineveh shall be overthrown." Nahum devotes three chapters detailing the coming destruction. Jonah's message was conditional. If Nineveh repented, then God would spare it. We know the Ninevites of that generation turned to God (Jonah 3). But there is now no hope for Nineveh. Nahum lashes out against this barbaric pagan people. Nineveh had ravaged the nations. God was going to obliterate it in His fiery judgment! The psalmist said the nation that forgets God will "return to Sheol" (Ps. 9:17). The ruins of ancient Nineveh, discovered in the mid-nineteenth century A.D., testify to this fact.

The Prophet's Name—Nahum

Nahum's name means *comfort* or *consolation*. He is the only one in the Old Testament record with this name. Though his message is doom for Nineveh, it would bring comfort to those nations oppressed by Nineveh—especially to remaining Judah (1:15). The northern kingdom had already been destroyed by the Assyrians in 722 BC.

Location of the Prophet—Elkosh (1:1)

Scholars have always debated the location of Elkosh. They have identified Elkosh with Capernaum in Galilee, with the village of Al-Kush near ancient Nineveh, and Elcesei, a village in Judah between Jerusalem and Gaza. Not knowing the exact location does not hinder our understanding of his message.

The Theme of the Book

The theme of Nahum is the predicted doom of Nineveh, capital of Assyria. The destruction of Nineveh in 612 BC at the hands of the Medes and the Neo-Babylonian empire was decreed by God: "'Behold, I am against you,' declares the LORD of hosts" (2:13). How utterly awful to have God be against us! Praise God for the comfort which comes from the apostle Paul: "If God is for us, who can be against us?" (Rom. 8:31b).

Time of Nahum's Ministry—Seventh Century BC

We know on the basis of 3:8-10 that Nahum prophesied in the seventh century BC. Nahum speaks of No-ammon (Thebes) as having been destroyed, and he predicts that Nineveh will be as well. Thebes was destroyed in 661 BC and Nineveh was destroyed in 612 BC. Thus Nahum must have prophesied between these two dates.

Summary of the Book

1. The Destruction of Nineveh Decreed (Chapter 1)

Nahum begins by giving us an awesome description of the God who has decreed to destroy the city (1:1-5). He then asks, "Who can stand before his indignation? Who can endure the heat of his anger?" (1:6). The answer is given in 1:7: "The LORD is good, a stronghold [fortress] in the day of trouble; he knows those who take refuge in him." Human fortresses will fall. The only refuge from the storms of judgment is God! He concludes the chapter by picturing the severity of the destruction (1:8-12a). This would be good news to Judah, which had suffered greatly under Assyria's domination (1:12b-15).

2. The Destruction of Nineveh Described (Chapter 2)

Remember that Nahum is seeing a vision of the destruction of Nineveh. We enter into the battle with him, but like Nahum we are just bystanders. We see the invader come up against the ancient citadel (2:1-3). We look right in on the siege: Chariots are raging in the streets (2:4); the army is fighting for the wall (2:5); the gates of the river are opened (2:6); captives are taken (2:7); people are fleeing (2:8); the city is sacked (2:9-10a); tremendous fear prevails (2:10b); and the leaders are defeated (under the figure of lions—2:11-12). A summary of the destruction is given in 2:13.

3. The Destruction of Nineveh Deserved (Chapter 3)

God did not act arbitrarily with Nineveh; He never does with any nation or individual. Nineveh's destruction came because it was deserved. When people and nations persistently violate the holiness of God, they will pay for it. Nineveh's sins were identified (3:1-7) and their punishment was assured (3:8-13). No defense would be successful (3:14-19).

Arrogance and boastfulness caused the downfall of Nineveh. The Bible teaches that pride comes before the fall. Zephaniah 2:15 describes Nineveh's pride and downfall: "This is the exultant city that lived securely, that said in her heart, 'I am, and there is no one else.' What a desolation she has become, a lair for wild beasts! Everyone who passes by her hisses and shakes his fist." How utterly awful is arrogance! Let us remember Peter's words on the subject of humility in 1 Peter 5:6.

ZEPHANIAH (SEVENTH CENTURY BC)

Do you know how to cry? Do you know what it is like to have great sorrow of heart? Have you had the experience of seeing something very precious to you fall apart? If you answer "yes," then you know what Zephaniah felt watching Judah corrupt itself into destruction. Zephaniah wanted to do something about it, so he lashed out against his people and leaders with an awesome message of coming judgment. He described his people as a nation that "knows no shame." He cried out that "the day of the Lord is near"—that day when God in fiery judgment would pour out His wrath on sinners. But though he painted a dark, dark picture through two-and-a-half chapters, he also did what all the other prophets did—he gave hope for the future (3:9-20). God is not finished with His ancient people. Someday God will establish them on the earth and will dwell in their midst!

The Prophet's Name—Zephaniah

Zephaniah's name means *Jehovah shall hide*, or *conceal*. There are four men in the Old Testament with this name. A play on the prophet's name occurs in 2:3: "Perhaps you may be hidden on the day of the anger of the LORD." The Bible pictures the Lord as a place of refuge and safety for His people (Col. 3:3). The poet has phrased it thus: "O safe and happy shelter, O refuge tried and sweet."

The Theme of the Book

The theme of the book is the judgment and blessing of God. Judgment is the subject of 1:1-3:8, and blessing of 3:9-20. The judgment is directed toward Judah and Jerusalem and several surrounding nations. All of these predictions were fulfilled to the letter except 3:8. The blessing aspect is for both Israel and the nations. It is still future in its fulfillment.

The International Situation

The Assyrians were getting closer to the end of their power over the nations. In 626 BC Nabopollassar, an Assyrian general who was in charge of Babylon, rebelled against the empire and became the founder of the Neo-Babylonian Empire. His son Nebuchadnezzar, later became king. The Neo-Babylonians, along with the Medes, invaded Nineveh and destroyed it in 612 BC. Zephaniah prophesied that the coming destruction of Judah and Jerusalem (1:4-2:3; 3:1-7) would come from the Babylonians.

The Babylonians invaded Judah three times (605, 597, and 586 BC) and carried off captives. The final time, they destroyed Jerusalem. All the preaching of Zephaniah, Habakkuk, and Jeremiah, plus the reforms of Josiah (2 Kings 22-23) could not turn the stiff-necked people of Judah back to God. They had passed the point of repentance, though God's gracious invitation was still extended.

The Location of the Prophet

Since Zephaniah was a relative of King Hezekiah (1:1) we infer that he lived and ministered in Jerusalem. He carried on his ministry during the reign of good King Josiah who ruled from 640–609 BC.

Summary of the Book

1. The Book Opens on the Theme of Judgment (1:1–3:8)

Zephaniah predicts the fall of Judah and Jerusalem. He predicts whom the judgment will affect (1:4-13), when it will come (1:14), what it will be like (1:15-17), and the fact that no one can escape (1:18–2:3).

From God's people he turns to the nations surrounding Palestine: Philistia, Ammon, Moab, and Assyria. They are denounced for their sin and threatened with judgment (2:4-15).

Zephaniah's spotlight returns to Jerusalem (3:1-7). The city is portrayed as utterly wicked (3:1-4), and in spite of God's presence with them (3:5), pursuing a path of shameful sin (3:6-7).

At this point, Zephaniah does what so many of the prophets do. They leave a situation where judgment is somewhat imminent and local and leap over the centuries to a time of judgment which is yet future and universal. Verse 8 refers to the battle of Armageddon, referred to in Joel 3:9-16 and Revelation 19:11-21. This final battle will come to its end when Jesus Christ comes to earth to put down all rule and authority. Then His kingdom will be established on the earth.

2. The Book Closes on the Theme of Blessing (3:9-10)

Zephaniah predicts the conversion of the nations (3:9-10) who will call upon the Lord in true and pure worship. The rest of the chapter predicts the conversion of the nation of Israel (3:11-20). In the past, Israel was characterized by shame, arrogance, unrighteousness, and fear of their enemies. "On that day" all will be changed, for they will have trust, holiness, righteousness and supreme joy. Verses 11-20 are some of the most positive and beautiful verses in the Bible. Read them and worship!

HABAKKUK (SEVENTH CENTURY BC)

For centuries, people have questioned the continued presence of evil in our world. Some have asked these questions from a skeptical point of view. They have not been people of faith. Habakkuk had his questions, too. However, he was not a doubter. He had a tremendously strong faith in God, but he was bewildered, perplexed, and outraged! He could not understand the seeming indifference of God in the face of all the wickedness and iniquity in Judah and Jerusalem. If God is a holy God, and if God knows what is going on in the nation, then why doesn't God do something about it?

Perhaps you have felt the same as Habakkuk, and perhaps you have become impatient. Habakkuk will teach us that God knows what He is doing, and that our part is to trust and submit to His wisdom and will.

The Prophet's Name

Habakkuk's name means *to embrace or to cling*. In a spiritual sense, this is exactly what he did in relation to God. The meaning of his name suggests his perseverance in holding fast to God in faith in spite of the puzzling questions which filled his mind. What a lesson for us! When we face problems, we need to cling to God in faith. We must not let the mystery of a situation overwhelm us to the point of doubt and despair. We must always remember that an all-wise and all-loving God is on the throne. He always does what is right!

The Location of the Prophet

Habakkuk was a prophet of Judah. His prophecy does not say that he lived in Jerusalem, but it can be safely inferred that he did. His mention of the moral and social evils best fits Jerusalem (1:1-4).The fact that the prayer psalm (3:1-19) was for the choir director (3:19) implies that he lived in Jerusalem.

The Theme of the Book

The theme is clearly the perplexing problems and prayer plea of a man of faith. This book is very helpful for any believer in Jesus Christ who has questions about how God responds to evil in society.

The Time of Habakkuk's Ministry

Generally, Habakkuk ministered during the time when the Neo-Babylonian Empire was a rising power. Though he does not mention a king in the beginning of his book, he does mention the rise of the Chaldeans (Neo-Babylonian empire) which began in 626 BC. Specifically, Habakkuk prophesied after the fall of Nineveh in 612 BC but before the first invasion of Judah by the Babylonians in 605 BC. Can we narrow it down even further? Yes. The moral and social wickedness which Habakkuk describes in 1:1-4 fits well the reign of Jehoiakim (see your chart) who ruled in Judah from 609 to 597 BC. The prophet Jeremiah gave a scathing indictment of Jehoiakim for his wickedness in Jeremiah 22:12-23.

Summary of the Book

1. The Perplexing Problems of a Man of Faith (1–2)

Problem—1:1-4

Why hadn't God done something about the awful moral depravity of Judah (1:1-4)? Habakkuk believed that God knew of the situation and could do something about it. Otherwise, he would not have prayed. But the prayer reveals his bewilderment. If God was as sensitive to sin as was Habakkuk, why hadn't He done something about it? Have you ever felt this way?

Solution—1:5-11

God is not indifferent to sin and He is at work to bring about changes. But God is sovereign. He has a plan and a timetable to execute His plan. He told Habakkuk that He was raising up the Chaldeans to punish Judah and Jerusalem. This answer was a staggering thought to Habakkuk and immediately raised a theological problem, as we shall see in the next point.

Problem—1:12-17

Instead of lifting Habakkuk's burden, God's solution to use the Babylonians added to it. How could God, who is holy, use a people more wicked than Judah as the rod of His punishment?

Solution—2:1-20

God does not always answer our perplexities in the way that we think He should. God leaves many questions unanswered, and our faith must respond. So be it! But a threefold answer is given to this man of faith:

1. The just shall live by faith (2:1-4)
2. The Babylonians' doom is assured (2:5-19)
3. The Sovereign Lord is ruling (2:20)

2. The Prayer Psalm of Habakkuk, the Man of Faith (3)

Habakkuk could complain no longer. But now he will open his mouth in prayer, not to complain, but to petition and praise.

His petition (3:1-2)

He prayed that God would show mercy in the process of bringing judgment. We know He did this because a remnant was spared from death. Later they came back to Palestine after the captivity to Babylon (3:1-2).

His vision (3:3-15)

After his petition, God gave Habakkuk a vision of a past event. It was a vision of the mighty power of God in the exodus from Egypt and the march to the Promised Land. God was with them and went before them in irresistible power. What is the point? Why would God give Habakkuk a vision of something which happened centuries before? The reason seems to be this: Just as God was invincible in leading His people to victory and judging the nations in the process, so now, because of Judah's sin, He will be invincible in leading Babylon against Judah and Jerusalem. Nothing can halt His march to accomplish His will. This vision had an awesome, yet wholesome effect on Habakkuk.

His Response (3:16-19)

The thought of God's fearsome judgment brought terror to his heart, but there was nothing he could do about it. It was God's will, so he simply accepted it and waited quietly for the judgment. His fear turned to exultation and exhilaration. What a lesson for us! Even in dark days we can have joy and exult in God. God will be our salvation. Let us give Him praise!

LESSON 8 EXAM

Use the exam sheet that has been provided to complete your exam.

1. **Jonah and Nahum both had in common**
   A. that they are both mentioned in 2 Kings.
   B. their tribal location in Palestine.
   C. their preaching against Nineveh.
   D. their family backgrounds.

2. **The theme of Nahum is**
   A. the comfort of Israel.
   B. the coming Messiah.
   C. the joy of salvation.
   D. the predicted doom of Nineveh.

3. **The time of Nahum's ministry was the**
   A. eighth century BC.   C. sixth century BC.
   B. seventh century BC.   D. fifth century BC.

4. **Zephaniah described the southern kingdom as a nation that**
   A. knew no shame.
   B. lost its hope.
   C. blamed God for its problems.
   D. sought God's mercy.

5. **Zephaniah's name means**
   A. "Jehovah shall hide, or conceal."
   B. "who is like Jehovah?"
   C. "Jehovah, my banner."
   D. "Jehovah casts off."

6. **The founder of the Neo-Babylonian empire was**
   A. Ashurbanipal.   C. Nebuchadnezzar.
   B. Nabopolassar.   D. Marduk.

7. **The theme of Zephaniah is**
   A. the doom of Nineveh.
   B. the judgment and blessing of God.
   C. the second coming of Christ.
   D. the conversion of the nations.

8. **Habakkuk's questions were evidence that he was**
   A. agnostic.
   B. atheistic.
   C. carnal.
   D. bewildered and perplexed.

9. **Habakkuk's first problem (1:1-4) had to do with why**
   A. God was punishing Judah.
   B. God was allowing the rise of the Neo-Babylonians.
   C. God had not done something about Judah's sin.
   D. God had been unjust in His treatment of Judah.

10. **Habakkuk closes his prophecy (chapter 3) with**
    A. a prediction of the coming messianic kingdom.
    B. a petition that God would have mercy on Judah.
    C. an exhortation to the southern kingdom to resist Babylon.
    D. a revelation that the just shall live by faith.

What Do You Say?

Habakkuk had his doubts and handled them appropriately. How have you handled yours?

Pre-Exilic Prophets (Part 5): Jeremiah and Lamentations

JEREMIAH

"The Wages of Sin is Death"

God did not give to any of us a blueprint of our lives when we became Christians. We can all appreciate both the wisdom and kindness of this. He did tell some of His servants, like Paul (Acts 9:14), that they would suffer greatly for His name. Jeremiah was one of those (Jer. 1:1-19). Jeremiah's message of condemnation and judgment was very unpopular. His audience hated what he preached and persecuted him severely. No Old Testament prophet suffered for his faith like Jeremiah. He was a holy man of God who would not compromise his personal life and ministry. The apostle Paul

> **God would be everything that Jeremiah needed in a time of danger and persecution.**

taught that "all [not just prophets] who desire to live a godly life in Christ Jesus will be persecuted" (2 Tim. 3:12). Jesus taught that "'a servant [slave] is not greater than his master.' If they persecuted me, they will also persecute you" (John 15:20; see also Matt. 5:10-12).

Jeremiah learned early that he had to fix his spiritual sight on God who had called him to such a trying ministry. God gave him many incentives not to give up, such as the promise of His presence, power, and reward (Jer. 1:1-19).

God told Jeremiah that he was not to be "dismayed" by his enemies or God would "dismay" him before them (1:17). God would be everything that he needed in a time of danger and persecution. The servant of Jesus Christ today needs to remember that he is not left to himself in doing God's will in difficult times. The Christian can expect the power of the Holy Spirit to accomplish God's will.

The Author of Jeremiah

Chapter 1 (1:1-3) reveals the author of this prophecy to be "Jeremiah, the son of Hilkiah, one of the priests who were in Anathoth in the land of Benjamin." Jeremiah mentioned his name approximately 130 times in his prophecy. In contrast, Isaiah used his name only sixteen times and Ezekiel just two times. His name means *Jehovah will lift up or exalt.* The names of the prophets often have prophetic significance for their ministries. Jeremiah's name was possibly meant to encourage him not to give up, for he would be exalted. Peter wrote in his first epistle, "Humble yourselves, therefore, under the mighty hand of God so that at the proper time he may exalt you, casting all your anxieties on him, because he cares for you" (1 Pet. 5:6-7).

The names of the prophets often have prophetic significance for their ministries.

Jeremiah came from the small village of Anathoth in the land of Benjamin (1:1). Anathoth was about three miles northeast of Jerusalem. It was a Levitical city (Josh. 21:18), a place where sons of the priests and Levites lived. Jesus taught that "no prophet is acceptable in his hometown" (Luke 4:24). This was certainly true of Jeremiah and the people of Anathoth. They hated Jeremiah so bitterly that they plotted to kill him (Jer. 11:18-23).

Like Isaiah, we do not know much of Jeremiah's family background. He was from a priestly family (1:1), though it appears that he did not minister as a priest. His father's name was Hilkiah and is not to be confused with the high priest during the time of good King Josiah (2 Kings 23:4). Jeremiah was not married before the destruction of Jerusalem (586 BC). God commanded him not to take a wife (16:2) because of the awful destruction which was to come upon families when the Babylonians invaded (16:3-9). In some sense, the singleness of Jeremiah was a sign to Judah and Jerusalem of the coming devastation. If people asked him why he had not married, his answer would be a warning to them!

The Call of Jeremiah to the Prophetic Ministry

The first chapter of Jeremiah records his call to serve as a prophet in Judah and Jerusalem. The following outline will summarize the important aspects of this call.

1. The Time of His Ministry (1:1-3)

Jeremiah ministered in the reigns of the last five Judean kings. He mentioned all of them in the course of his prophesying.

Josiah was a very godly king, but the others were evil. Jeremiah began his ministry in the thirteenth year of Josiah (627 BC). He continued past the destruction of Jerusalem (586 BC) as is indicated in chapters 39–52.

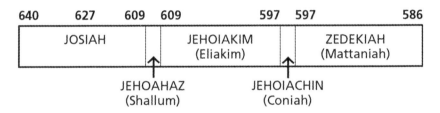

2. The Appointment to His Ministry (1:4-5)

The text points out that God had planned his future before he was born. This would emphasize that God had first claim on his life.

3. The Scope of His Ministry (1:5b, 10a)

His prophecies would address the nation, not just Israel. Chapters 46–51 record prophecies against such nations as Egypt and Babylon.

4. Jeremiah's Response to His Call (1:6)

He strongly complained that he did not know how to speak and that he was only a youth. We can all identify with such inadequacy. But we should not use it as an excuse!

5. God's Encouragement to Jeremiah (1:7-8)

After commanding Jeremiah not be preoccupied with his weaknesses (1:7a), God encouraged him to let fear be displaced by trust (Prov. 3:5-6), "for I am with you to deliver you ..." (1:8). God's presence with us is an antidote to many negative influences in our lives (Heb. 13:5).

6. The Empowerment in His Ministry (1:9)

"Then the Lord put out his hand and touched my mouth. And the Lord said to me, 'Behold, I have put my words in your mouth.'" The touching of Jeremiah's mouth, in contrast to Isaiah's experience (Isa. 6:6-7), symbolized new power from God for communication. Whatever gift God gives, He will enable its effective use.

7. The Nature of His Ministry (1:10)

Jeremiah's ministry would be both negative and positive. The negative is seen with the words "pluck up ... break down ... destroy and ... overthrow." The positive is seen with the words "to build and to plant" (see Jer. 31:27-30). His messages would deal with both judgment and salvation. The emphasis, however, was on judgment.

8. The Visions of His Ministry (1:11-16)

God gave to Jeremiah two visions that foretold judgment upon Judah—the almond tree (1:11-12) and the boiling pot (1:13-16). These visions teach that God, in His time, would fulfill His word of judgment and that his judgment would be very severe when it came.

9. The Warning of His Ministry (1:17)

This was referred to in the introduction. Jeremiah must not rebel against his call or God would discipline him.

10. The Promise to Him as He Ministers (1:18-19)

God promised to make Jeremiah so strong that his enemies could not overcome him (1:18a). The metaphors of "a fortified city ... iron pillar, and bronze walls" illustrate the strength of Jeremiah if he would obey. We know by the way the book ends that, though he was treated very badly, his enemies did not triumph over him. God always keeps His word of promise! You, too, can count on the power of His presence in your life and ministry (Matt. 28:20b; Acts 1:8).

The Structure of Jeremiah

Introduction	Jeremiah's ministry	Jeremiah's ministry	Conclusion
Jeremiah's call to the ministry	concerning Judah and Jerusalem	concerning the surrounding nations	Historical appendix
1	2-45	46-51	52

Chapter 1 describes the dynamic call of Jeremiah to the prophetic ministry. God clearly told him of the origin, responsibilities, empowerment, and possible success of his ministry.

Chapters 2–45 deal with the sins of the southern kingdom. In spite of God's incredible love for His people, they had forsaken Him. Jeremiah 2:13 summarizes the apostasy of the nation: "For my people have committed two evils: they have forsaken me, the fountain of living waters, and hewed out cisterns for themselves, broken cisterns that can hold no water." "Broken cisterns" represents the nation's idolatry (2:12-13) and foreign alliances (2:17-18). Just as broken cisterns cannot supply water, so the nation's rebellion cannot provide them with protection and stability. Only God, the "fountain of living waters," can do that. Jeremiah, by sermons and by signs, calls the nation to repentance.

Jeremiah is an apt picture of our Lord Jesus Christ in His suffering and ministry.

Even though it was the eleventh hour of their history and judgment was knocking at their door, there was still time to return to the Lord (3:1, 12, 14, 22; 4:1, 4, 14; 5:1). But Jeremiah exclaims, "They refused to take correction. They have made their faces harder than rock; they have refused to repent" (5:3b).

Jeremiah's message to the last four kings of Judah was extremely unpopular. He preached submission to the Babylonians (chapter 27) because otherwise Jerusalem would be destroyed and the nation would go into captivity (exile) for seventy years (22:5-10; 25:8-11). Both the leaders of Jerusalem and the common people hated Jeremiah for this and plotted his death (26:7-24)—a plot that was not successful. Throughout these many chapters, Jeremiah was mocked, ridiculed, falsely accused, rejected, threatened, hunted, physically abused, imprisoned, and starved (11:18-23; 18:18; 20:1-3; 26:7-24; 36; 37:11–38:13). His soul was often in anguish

(4:19-26; 8:18-22; 13:17; 15:18; 20:7-18). It is no wonder that he is called the "man of sorrows" and "the weeping prophet." He is an apt picture of our Lord Jesus Christ in His suffering and ministry (Isa. 53:2-3).

Though most of this section (chapters 2–45) deals with judgment fulfilled in the past, there are a few references to the Messiah and His kingdom. Let us observe two outstanding passages.

1. The New Covenant (31:31-34)

This passage consists of five provisions of the new covenant.

1.   *The People of the New Covenant.* God will make a new covenant with Judah and Israel. However, we in the present church age will experience some of the benefits of this covenant—a covenant made in Jesus' blood (Matt. 26:26-29).

2.   *The Nature of the New Covenant.* It is entirely unconditional in nature (contrast the old covenant, which depended on man's obedience). The fulfillment of this covenant depends entirely on God.

3.   *The Motivation of the New Covenant.* God will do a work by His power in the hearts of His people which will enable them to live for Him (compare Rom. 8).

4.   *The Relationship of the New Covenant.* It is a spiritual relationship, not external. God said, "I will be their God, and they shall be my people ... They shall all know me, from the least of them to the greatest."

5.   *The Basis of the New Covenant.* The basis is the grace of God in forgiveness: "For I will forgive their iniquity, and I will remember their sin no more." Christ's sacrifice made this possible.

2. The King and the Kingdom (23:3-8)

These verses are surrounded by the condemnation of the rulers of Jeremiah's day (chapters 22–23). These rulers were incredibly wicked. But someday in the future a King will come who will establish the kingdom, and righteousness will prevail. Let us observe some things about this coming Messiah in verses 5-6: His origin is in the line of David. His character is righteous in every way (morally, ethically, and religiously). His rule will be characterized by wisdom, righteousness, and justice. His blessing will include salvation and preservation (dwell securely). His name (and thus His identity) is The Lord our righteousness. A great day is ahead when "the sun of righteousness shall rise with healing in its wings" (Mal. 4:2).

Chapters 46-51 form the second major section of Jeremiah. Like Isaiah and Ezekiel, Jeremiah describes the judgment to come on the nations surrounding Palestine: Egypt (chapter 46), Philistia (chapter 47), Moab (chapter 48), Ammon (49:1-6), Edom (49:7-22), Syria (49:23-27), Kedar and Hazor (49:28-33), Elam (49:34-39), and Babylon (chapters 50–51). All of these prophecies have been fulfilled in history with the exception of some of the prophecy concerning Babylon. Some of the statements concerning Babylon parallel those made in Revelation 18, where the future destruction of Babylon is foretold.

Chapter 52 is the conclusion to the book and reads somewhat like a historical appendix. It recounts the fall of Jerusalem already given in chapter 39. The nation of Babylon which would one day be destroyed (chapters 50–51) was not in control of Judah and Jerusalem. It was God who used Babylon to inflict punishment upon His backslidden people (Hab. 1).

Some General Observations about Jeremiah

- Although Jeremiah has fewer chapters than Isaiah, it has more content. That makes it the longest of the prophets.
- It is a book that is topical in arrangement rather than chronological.
- It is a book that is vital to understanding 2 Kings chapters 22-25.
- It is a book filled with sadness and anguish that results from sin.
- It is a book which is more autobiographical than all the other prophets put together.
- It is a book that contains very little messianic prophecy, but what it has offers bright hope for the future of Israel.

LAMENTATIONS

This is the book of Jeremiah's tears! He wrote this little book after the capture and destruction of Jerusalem at the hands of the Babylonians in 586 BC. It is five tear-filled poems expressing the prophet's great grief over the desolation of Jerusalem. The book also shows the unconditional love of God for His people. On the one hand we see His sorrow for the very ones He was punishing. On the other hand we see His great mercy, which is Israel's only hope of restoration (3:21-26).

The Structure of the Book

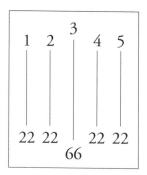

Chapters 1, 2, 4, and 5 have twenty-two verses each, and chapter 3 has sixty-six (3 x 22). There are twenty-two letters in the Hebrew alphabet, and the first four chapters each form an alphabetic acrostic. Chapter five, for some unknown reason, was not built on an acrostic structure.

Let us take chapter 1, for example. The first word of verse 1 begins with the first letter of the Hebrew alphabet (*aleph*). The first word of the second verse begins with the second letter of the alphabet (*beth*), and so on.

This process is tripled in chapter 3 with its sixty-six verses so that the first words of the first three verses begin with *aleph*. Acrostics were used in the Bible as memory devices.

The Content of Lamentations

The First Lamentation (Chapter 1)

The city of Jerusalem was depicted by Jeremiah as a sorrowful and weeping widow. Jeremiah personified Jerusalem as having sorrow greater than any other (1:12).

The Second Lamentation (Chapter 2)

This chapter pictures Jerusalem as a woman veiled with the cloud of God's wrath (2:1). There is no doubt that the reason for Jerusalem's destruction is the nation's awful sin. God has righteously visited the city with deserved judgment.

The Third Lamentation (Chapter 3)

In this chapter Jeremiah describes the afflictions of Jerusalem as if they were his own sufferings. Here we see the greatness of Jeremiah's heart as he identifies with and mourns the afflictions of God's people. Through the blur of his tears he is able to see the prospect of the loving-kindness and mercy of God (3:22-54).

The Fourth Lamentation (Chapter 4)

This lamentation is heartbreaking as it describes the awful siege conditions in the city. It is so awful that women have cooked their own children for food! This kind of thing happened during the Nazi siege of Leningrad during the Second World War.

The Fifth Lamentation (Chapter 5)

After the Babylonians destroyed Jerusalem, they left behind a remnant of Jewish people to inhabit the land. Jeremiah was one of them. Strictly speaking, this chapter is their prayer for God's intervention on their behalf (5:1). Jeremiah cries out to God, "Remember, O Lord, what has befallen us; look, and see our disgrace!" This prayer is based on all that they were presently suffering (5:2-18).

Some Lessons from Lamentations

One of the most prominent lessons of this book is that when the people of God persist in sin, the result is divine judgment. Israel was a rebellious nation that reaped what it sowed.

Another important lesson involves the compassion and grace of God. No matter how far one goes in sin, God will always forgive and restore the repentant believer. It was on this basis that Jeremiah prayed his prayer in chapter 5 (compare Rom. 5:20-21). Let us keep our lives in constant fellowship with our God and with one another so that our song is one of joy and not a lament!

LESSON 9 EXAM

Use the exam sheet that has been provided to complete your exam.

1. **Jeremiah, a priest, was from the Levitical city of**
   A. Golan.
   B. Anathoth.
   C. Bethel.
   D. Hebron.

2. **God commanded Jeremiah not to take a wife because**
   A. he would be distracted from his ministry.
   B. he would not make a suitable husband.
   C. of the awful death and destruction to come.
   D. of the shortness of life.

3. **"Broken cisterns" is a metaphor standing for Judah's**
   A. brokenness before God.
   B. idolatry and foreign alliances.
   C. drought conditions.
   D. economic problems.

4. **The vast majority of the content of chapters 2-45 deals with**
   A. judgment which was fulfilled in the past.
   B. a balance of judgment and blessing fulfilled in the past.
   C. the future judgment in the tribulation period.
   D. the future kingdom of God.

5. **One of the provisions of the new covenant is**
   A. its unconditional nature.
   B. its self-empowered motivation.
   C. its basis in man's efforts.
   D. its external relationship.

6. **One general observation about Jeremiah is that**
   A. it is the longest book of the prophets.
   B. it is vital to understanding Ezra and Nehemiah.
   C. its prophecies are arranged in chronological order.
   D. it is a book with a lot of messianic prophecy.

7. **Some of the prophecies concerning Babylon (Jeremiah 50-51) parallel statements made in**
   A. Romans.
   B. 1 Thessalonians.
   C. Hebrews.
   D. Revelation.

8. **Jeremiah described the character of the coming Messiah as**
   A. faithful.
   B. loving.
   C. powerful.
   D. righteous.

9. **Jeremiah wrote the book of Lamentations**
   A. before the revival in Josiah's time.
   B. during the kingship of Jehoiakim.
   C. after the capture and destruction of Jerusalem.
   D. toward the beginning of Jerusalem's restoration.

10. **Jeremiah depicted Jerusalem in the first lamentation as**
    A. an estranged widow.
    B. a weeping widow.
    C. a veiled woman.
    D. a taunting woman.

What Do You Say?

Think about Jeremiah 2:13. Do you have a testimony of "broken cisterns" in your past? How did you get rid of them?

_____

_____

_____

_____

EXAM 9

Exilic Prophets (Part 1): Daniel

The Prophet of the Times of the Gentiles

One of the most difficult things for people of all ages to cope with is great or sudden change. Illness, death in the family, divorce, and great economic loss require significant character to cope. Some people collapse under the strain. But these are elements God uses to build character in the lives of those who know Him (James 1:2-4). James encourages us to "let steadfastness have its full effect, that you may be perfect and complete, lacking in nothing."

Daniel was one of those prophets who knew about great change. Chapter 1 of his book describes his experience. He was just a youth torn away from family and country and taken far away to a pagan land and culture. He had to serve in a pagan court, minister to pagan kings, and learn a new language and literature. His name was changed to a name that reflected paganism (Belteshazzar).

> **Daniel had been taught to worship the one true God.**

One change he reacted to was the change in his diet. To eat of the king's food would have violated his religious conviction. He respectfully requested a change in diet, which was granted.

Daniel had to learn to cope with his change and he did. How? It was through his trust in God. In times of tragedy, people often look to a "higher power." Daniel had been taught to worship the one true God. More than at any other time in his life, he "cast [his] burden on the LORD" (Ps. 55:22), and God sustained him. He did not know what an incredible life the Lord had planned for him in Babylon. Because Daniel knew that God never changes, he was able to cope with the changing situations of his life. The results were wonderful, for God used him mightily.

Daniel, the Man

His Personal History

Family Background

Daniel, which means *God is my judge*, did not give any family information about himself. We know that he was a youth who may have been a part of the royal family of David (1:3-4).

A Historical Person

The Bible makes it quite clear in both the Old and New Testaments (Ezek. 14:14, 20; 28:3; Matt. 24:15) that Daniel was a genuine historical figure. Liberal critics of the book of Daniel view Daniel as a fictional character.

His Character

The character of Daniel ranks with other great men of God like Moses, Abraham, and Joseph. Very likely his upbringing had been a great factor in his virtuous life. He was a man of strong and uncompromising religious convictions (1:8); a man of prayer and worship (2:17-23; 6:10); a person of genuine humility (2:28-30); an honest public official (6:4, 22); and a person of tremendous courage, as seen when he confronted King Nebuchadnezzar (chapter 4) and King Belshazzar (chapter 5).

His Intellectual Capacity

King Nebuchadnezzar was very impressed with Daniel's wisdom and understanding. He said, after examining Daniel and his three friends, that they were ten times better than all the wise men of his court (1:20). Daniel was consistent, however, in attributing his ability to God (1:17).

His Position in the Court

Daniel was a civil officer in the court of the Babylonian and Persian kings. Though he did not have the prophetic office, he did have the prophetic gift, and he used it for the praise and honor of God. With it he was able to have a powerful influence on two gentile kings, Nebuchadnezzar and

Darius the Mede. Always bear in mind, however, that it was God who brought Daniel into his position of power. It was God who protected him from the hatred of jealous men (6:1-15) and the teeth of lions (6:16-24).

The Ministry of Daniel

Its Length

Daniel's ministry stretched over a very long period of time (605–536 BC). This period is determined by the time references in the book (1:1; 10:1)—the first year of Nebuchadnezzar to the third year of Cyrus. In other words, his ministry spanned the entire period of the Babylonian exile.

The Contemporary Prophets

Jeremiah and Ezekiel were contemporary with Daniel. Jeremiah prophesied in Jerusalem from 627 to 586 BC. Ezekiel prophesied in Tel-Abib (50 miles south of the city of Babylon) from 593 to 570 BC. Jeremiah was both a pre-exilic (627–605 BC) and an exilic prophet (605–586 BC). Daniel and Ezekiel were exilic prophets only.

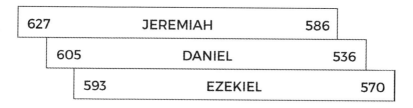

Historic Background

In 605 BC, Nebuchadnezzar led the Babylonians to invade Judah and Jerusalem and brought God's people into subjection. Jehoiachin was retained as the Jewish king, and captives were taken back to Babylon. Daniel was one of them (2 Kings 24:1; Dan. 1:1-4). In 597 BC, the Babylonians invaded again. They removed Jehoiachin from the kingship and carried off ten thousand captives (2 Kings 24:10-16). Ezekiel was one of them. The Babylonians installed a new king, Zedekiah, who ruled Judah for eleven years. In 586 BC (Zedekiah's eleventh year), the Babylonians destroyed Jerusalem and carried off more captives. Jeremiah was given the option of staying in the land or going to Babylon. He chose to stay (Jer. 40:1-6).

Daniel, The Book

Structure

The historical section of Daniel 1-6	The prophetical section of Daniel 7-12
A. Daniel and his three friends placed in the Babylonian court 1	A. Daniel's vision of the four beasts and the Ancient of Days 7
B. Daniel interpreted the great dream-image of Nebuchadnezzar 2	B. Daniel's vision of the ram and the he-goat 8
C. Daniel's three friends preserved in the fiery furnace 3	C. Daniel's vision of the prophecy of the seventy weeks 9
D. Daniel interpreted the three dreams of Nebuchadnezzar 4	D. Daniel's vision of the spiritual conflict in the unseen realm of spirits 10
E. Daniel interpreted the handwriting of the wall for King Belshazzar 5	E. Daniel's vision of the kings of the North and South 11
F. Daniel was preserved from the lions 6	F. Daniel's vision of the preservation and deliverance of God's people 12

Content

There is quite a contrast in the content of the two major sections of the book of Daniel:

1-6	7-12
1. Primarily history	1. Primarily prophecy
2. Daniel and his three friends	2. Daniel only
3. Just one brief passage on the future	3. Every chapter has prophecy the future
4. Daniel interacting with kings and dignitaries	4. Daniel interacting with God and angels
5. Daniel interpreting someone else's dream	5. Daniel interpreting his own dream-vision
6. Section inspires faith and perseverance through godly example	6. Section inspires faith and perseverance through prophetic revelations

Language

The book of Daniel was written in two languages—Hebrew and Aramaic. Note the breakdown:

HEBREW	ARAMAIC	HEBREW
1-2:4a	2:4b-7:28	8-12

Aramaic was the common language of the Near East. Many Jewish people learned to speak it while in exile. We do not know for certain why two languages were used. Some scholars have speculated that the Aramaic portion was directed to the Gentiles, emphasizing judgment. The Hebrew portions may have been directed to the Jewish people to inspire future hope and consolation. The use of both languages certainly illustrates the broad universal appeal of the book.

The Theme of the Book—The Times of the Gentiles and the Future Messianic Kingdom

The term "times of the Gentiles" is found in Luke 21:24: "They will fall by the edge of the sword and be led captive among all nations, and Jerusalem will be trampled underfoot by the Gentiles, until the times of the Gentiles are fulfilled."

The "times of the Gentiles" began with Nebuchadnezzar (605 BC) and will end with the literal second coming of Jesus Christ to the earth. Daniel traces the rise and fall of the first four Gentile world rulers—Babylon, Medo-Persia, Greece, and Rome (chapter 2). Jesus will put down the last Gentile world ruler (the Antichrist) and establish His own kingdom. This term is a political expression and is not to be confused with the phrase "fullness of the Gentiles" (Rom. 11:25). The fullness of the Gentiles refers to the salvation of Gentiles during the present church age.

Conclusion

One important lesson Daniel teaches us is the sovereign control of God over the nations of the world. God is not sitting on the edge of His chair in a state of confusion wondering what will happen to this sinful planet. He is in control! Nebuchadnezzar had it right when he said, "For his dominion is an everlasting dominion, and his kingdom endures from generation to generation; all the inhabitants of the earth are accounted as nothing, *and he does according to his will among the host of heaven and among the inhabitants of the earth; and none can stay his hand or say to him, "What have you done?"* (4:34-35 emphasis added). For our comfort and encouragement we must view the world and its events from the perspective of God's control. He is in charge and we can trust Him whatever comes.

LESSON 10 EXAM

Use the exam sheet that has been provided to complete your exam.

1. **Daniel was a genuine historical person as witnessed**
   A. by Ezekiel and Matthew.
   B. by Acts and 1 Peter.
   C. by 1 Corinthians and Romans.
   D. by 1 & 2 Timothy.

2. **King Nebuchadnezzar was impressed with Daniel's**
   A. physical appearance.
   B. intellectual capacity.
   C. moral uprightness.
   D. spiritual perception.

3. **Daniel's ministry covered the years**
   A. 636-570 BC.   C. 586-539 BC.
   B. 605-536 BC.   D. 581-516 BC.

4. **Daniel was a contemporary prophet of**
   A. Habakkuk.   C. Ezekiel.
   B. Nahum.   D. Malachi.

5. **The book of Daniel was written in two languages:**
   A. Hebrew and Syrian.
   B. Babylonian and Assyrian.
   C. Aramaic and Hebrew.
   D. Egyptian and Greek.

6. **The theme of Daniel is**
   A. the strength of the nations and the kingdom of God.
   B. the fullness of the Gentiles and the future messianic kingdom.
   C. the times of the Gentiles and the future messianic kingdom.
   D. the devastation of the Gentiles and God's kingdom.

7. **The structure of Daniel consists of**
   A. two major sections.
   B. three major sections.
   C. four major sections.
   D. six major sections.

8. **Daniel's name means**
   A. "God is my witness."
   B. "God is my honor."
   C. "God is my sufficiency."
   D. "God is my judge."

9. **Daniel served as a civil officer for the Babylonians in**
   A. Carchemish.   C. Damascus.
   B. Tel-abib.   D. Babylon.

10. **The "times of the Gentiles" began with Babylon and will continue until**
    A. the restoration from the Babylon captivity.
    B. the first advent of Jesus Christ.
    C. the rapture of the church to heaven.
    D. the second advent of Christ to earth.

What Do You Say?

How have you handled momentous changes in your life (remember Daniel 1)?

_____

_____

_____

_____

Exilic Prophets (Part 2): Ezekiel

The Prophet of the Glory of God

We live in a wonderful country. It is a land of opportunity, wealth, comfort, and freedom. We appreciate our democratic form of government. We would never want to give up those basic freedoms of speech, press, and religion. But have you ever thought how you would feel if we lost all of these precious freedoms? If you can imagine what that might be like, then you can identify with those whom Ezekiel addressed.

Israel in the captivity had lost their king, their land, their capital city, their worship system, and their national existence. They were a very discouraged people. They had given up hope (37:11) even though Jeremiah had prophesied that the exile would only last seventy years (Jer. 25, 29). Psalm 137 expresses their depression: "By the waters of Babylon, there we sat down and wept, when we remembered Zion. On the willows there we hung up our lyres. For there

> **It is easier to encourage than it is to confront, but God has called us to do both.**

our captors required of us songs, and our tormentors, mirth, saying, 'Sing us one of the songs of Zion!' How shall we sing the LORD's song in a foreign land?" (137:1-4).

But they were not only a discouraged people; they were also a rebellious people. Ezekiel was not only an encourager but he was also a watchman calling them back to a life of trust and righteousness (compare 2:1-10 with 3:16-21). He confronted them with messages of the judgment that would fall on Jerusalem. And he encouraged them with messages of hope and restoration. It is easier to encourage than it is to confront, but God has called us to do both.

Ezekiel, the Man

His Name

Ezekiel means *God will strengthen*, and he is the only one in the Old Testament by that name. He needed the power of God for the awesome task of ministering to the house of Israel. His name was a constant reminder that his God would supply all that was needed for him to fulfill his ministry.

His Title "Son of Man"

Throughout the book, God calls Ezekiel by the term "son of man." This expression simply means "mortal man." It must not be confused with the messianic title of Jesus as The Son of Man. Ezekiel's title would always remind him of his own weakness and of his need to depend upon God.

Personal History

Like the other prophets, we do not know a lot about Ezekiel's family background. His father, Buzi (1:3), was a priest. Ezekiel had a wife who died in exile (24:15-20). He must have had a good relationship with her, for she is spoken of as "the desire of [his] eyes" (24:15). Her death occurred nine years after Ezekiel and his family were taken to Babylon. Her death, and Ezekiel's response to it, was a sign to Israel of the coming destruction of Jerusalem and its temple (24:18-27).

His Exile History

Ezekiel lived in the community of Tel-Abib on the river Chebar where Nebuchadnezzar had settled the Jewish captives (3:15). He had his own house (3:24; 8:1) where the elders of Judah often visited him. Ezekiel favored the Babylonians for he knew God willed that the Jewish people should be in the captivity. Besides being a foreteller of future events, God also called him to a pastoral ministry among the exiles (chapters 3 and 33). He was to warn them to put away their wickedness and live righteously.

Ezekiel was unable to speak unless Jehovah had a message to pass on to the exiles (3:26-27). He regained his normal speech ability after the destruction of Jerusalem (compare 24:25-27 with 33:21-22). Spiritually, he was quite alone. The respect the elders showed Ezekiel was superficial (14:1-5). Even after the fall of Jerusalem, the respect of the people was still hypocritical (33:30-33). Genuine ministry for God will not always have the people's respect.

Ezekiel's Ministry

When He Ministered

Ezekiel ministered from the fifth year of King Jehoiachin's captivity to the twenty-seventh year (1:1; 29:17-30:19)—593–570 BC. His ministry lasted for twenty-two years, which was about half that of Jeremiah's (622–586 BC). Ezekiel, Jeremiah, and Daniel were contemporaries. While Ezekiel was ministering in a very rugged setting in Tel-Abib, Daniel was prophesying in the court of kings in Babylon. God places His servants where He wants them and gives them the particular ministry in which they engage. He promises strength to accomplish the task, whatever it is.

605 BC	597 BC	586 BC	536 BC
The 70-year Babylon Captivity			

593   570
Ezekiel's Ministry

His Commission (1–3)

God's commission began with Ezekiel's vision of the awesome glory of God (chapter 1). He saw a gigantic storm cloud out of which proceeded a heavenly chariot. In the Old Testament a storm cloud is often a symbol of judgment, and that is how it should be understood here. The chariot represented God coming to war against His people in judgment for their sins.

Ezekiel was overwhelmed by what he saw and fell on his face (1:28). The Lord commanded him to stand, and then He filled him with the Holy Spirit (2:1-2) so that he might have power to minister to the rebellious house of Israel (2:3–3:15). Ezekiel's commission closes with his appointment to a pastoral ministry ("watchman"): "Son of man, I have made you a watchman for the house of Israel. Whenever you hear a word from my mouth, you shall give them warning from me." (3:17). In a sense, all of us have a shepherding ministry to other believers (Gal. 6:1).

This marvelous vision of the glory of God is the most intricate in all the Old Testament. Ezekiel saw it several more times (3:22-23; 8:2-4; 10:1-22; 11:22-23; 43:1-6; 44:4), and it sustained him in the difficulties of his ministry. We may not have visions today as the biblical men of faith had, but we can "see" our glorious Lord each day in the pages of Scripture. What a privilege! Be occupied with Him!

Ezekiel, the Book

The Structure

Prophecies of judgment against Judah and Jerusalem	Prophecies of judgment against the nations	Prophecies of future restoration and glory for Israel
1–24	25–32	33–48
Given before the siege of Jerusalem	Given during the siege of Jerusalem	Given after the destruction of Jerusalem
593-588	588-586	586-570

The Content

1. Chapters 1–24

These are messages of judgment against Judah and Jerusalem with one exception (21:28-32). They were given from the fifth to the ninth year of King Jehoiachin's captivity (593–588 BC). All of these prophecies have been fulfilled with three exceptions (11:13-20; 20:33-44; 16:60-63). Ezekiel used a variety of methods in communicating God's revelation: (1) signs (4:1-3; 5:1-4; 12:1-13); (2) proverbs (12:22; 12:27; 18:2); (3) allegory (15:1-8; 17:1-21); and (4) direct preaching (20:1-49). Twenty-nine times in these chapters Ezekiel uses the expression, "you shall know that I am the LORD." By this he means that when the prophecies are fulfilled, Israel will know that it was through the sovereign power and control of God.

2. Chapters 25–32

These chapters contain judgment messages against the nations which immediately surround Palestine. They were the enemies of God's ancient people (Ammon, Moab, Edom, Philistia, Tyre, Sidon, and Egypt). All of these messages were fulfilled in the ancient past. The structure of these chapters is simple: the sin of each nation is pointed out and their punishment is foretold.

The purpose of the judgment is clearly given: "Then they will know that I am the LORD" (used twenty-four times in this section). One highlight of this section is the mention of the fall of Satan (28:11-19). Another is the description of Tyre using the figure of a ship with its various parts (chapter 27).

3. Chapters 33–48

This is the most glorious part of Ezekiel's prophecy. It begins with the recommission of Ezekiel (chapter 33). It then proceeds to detail the restoration of Israel to its land and blessings (chapters 34–39). Finally it closes with a description of the future millennial temple, worship, and land division (chapters 40–48). It is true that Israel was restored to its land after the Babylonian captivity, but these chapters deal with the future and give an outline of how God will bring it about.

Seventeen times in this section Ezekiel uses the expression "Then they will know that I am the LORD." It has the same meaning here as in the first two divisions.

Conclusion

There was much discouragement among the Jewish exiles to whom Ezekiel ministered. They were saying, "Our bones are dried up, and our hope is lost; we are indeed cut off" (37:11). This depression and discouragement is more mournfully described in Psalm 137. Ezekiel's antidote was to share the great vision of the glorious future of Israel. There is hope! There are glory days ahead! God is not through with His people! He will fulfill all His promises! God ministers to us in the same way when we are discouraged and depressed. Let us keep looking up to Him for His peace and joy in the adverse circumstances of life.

LESSON 11 EXAM

Use the exam sheet that has been provided to complete your exam.

1. **The people to whom Ezekiel was sent to minister in the Babylonian captivity were a**
   A. discouraged and rebellious people.
   B. distressed but confident people.
   C. submissive and compliant people.
   D. spiritual and discerning people.

2. **Throughout the book, God calls Ezekiel**
   A. "The Son of Man."
   B. "son of man."
   C. "the son of sorrow."
   D. "son of contentment."

3. **What was Ezekiel's physical condition through the first 32 chapters of the book?**
   A. He was made blind.
   B. He was made deaf.
   C. He was made mute.
   D. He was made lame.

4. **Ezekiel's messages are dated after the captivity of King**
   A. Jehoiakim.   C. Zedekiah.
   B. Jehoahaz.   D. Jehoiachin.

5. **Ezekiel's place of ministry in the captivity was in**
   A. Haran.   C. Tel-Abib.
   B. Babylon.   D. Susa.

6. **The term God used to designate the pastoral aspect of Ezekiel's ministry was**
   A. seer.   C. servant of God.
   B. watchman.   D. shepherd.

7. **Twenty-nine times in the first 24 chapters of Ezekiel, he used the expression**
   A. "the hand of the LORD was upon me."
   B. "that glory of the LORD."
   C. "that they may know that I am the LORD."
   D. "there is no peace to the wicked."

8. **What did Ezekiel see in his vision which represented God coming to war against His people?**
   A. A man with a sword.
   B. A chariot.
   C. A city under siege.
   D. A heavenly army.

9. **Ezekiel's ministry covered a period of**
   A. 40 years.   C. 27 years.
   B. 36 years.   D. 22 years.

10. **One of the highlights of chapters 25-32 is the mention of**
    A. the return from the Babylonian captivity.
    B. the great future restoration of Israel to their land.
    C. the fall of Satan.
    D. the 1,000-year kingdom of God.

What Do You Say?

How do you handle people that oppose you regarding your faith in Christ?

Post-Exilic Prophets: Haggai, Zechariah, Malachi

HAGGAI (SIXTH CENTURY BC)

Repent! Get right with God! Put first things first! Then God will be glorified and you will be blessed. That's the story of Haggai. But from what are they to repent? What must be at the top of their priority list?

In Habakkuk, we left God's people on the verge of the Babylonian captivity. But in Haggai, the captivity in Babylon is over and the people had returned to their land. They had made an attempt to put first things first. They started to build God's top priority project—the temple. In faith they built the altar and laid the foundation (Ezra 3); but when adverse circumstances arose in which they did not exercise faith (Ezra 4), fear dominated them, they stopped their building project, and they became preoccupied with materialism (Hag. 1:2-4). So they went from faith, to fear, to materialism! This is a familiar pattern that has hindered the church in various parts of the world over the last two thousand years.

Haggai rebuked the people, calling them back to devotion to the Lord and pursuit of their responsibility to rebuild the temple. His strong prophetic preaching was successful. We need more strong preaching to the church which seems to have the same sinful preoccupation with materialism. There is nothing wrong with having wealth, but it is sinful to have it at the expense of the work of the Lord.

The Prophet's Name—Haggai

Haggai's name means *festal* or *festive*. The first three letters (*hag*) form the Hebrew word for *feast* in the Old Testament. We do not know the significance of his name, but some think he was named Haggai because he was born on one of the great feast days of Israel. Others think his name simply refers to joy. It is interesting that when Haggai preached his second sermon (2:1), it was preached on the last day of the Feast of Tabernacles, the most joyous feast of the Jewish people. The completion of the rebuilding of the temple was a time of great festive joy for the restored people of God.

Location of the Prophet

It is quite clear from both Ezra (Ezra 5:1-2) and Haggai, that Haggai was a prophet of Judah and Jerusalem. He began his ministry "in the second year of Darius the king, in the sixth month, on the first day of the month," and one of the receivers of his message was Zerubbabel the son of Shealtiel, who was governor in Judah. (521 BC—see chart in lesson 5).

The Theme of the Book

The theme of Haggai is very simple and practical. It is the rebuilding of the Jewish temple by the exiles who returned from Babylon. Remember that this is the theme of Ezra 1–6, which provides the historic background for Haggai. Addressing this theme, Haggai gave four messages.

Summary of the Book

The four messages were meant to exhort, to stir up, and to motivate to action. The prediction of future events (2:6-9; 2:20-22) is given for the purpose of encouragement. The messages were preached over a period of four months (see chart on next page). Zechariah, a companion prophet of Haggai, preached some of his messages during the same period. You can observe where Zechariah's first two messages fit in with Haggai's ministry. Remember that this ministry began in the second year of Darius I.

1. The *first message* (1:1-15) was given to rebuke the carnal citizens of Judah and Jerusalem and to stimulate them to get back to their first duty of rebuilding the temple. It was successful.
2. The *second message* (2:1-9) was meant to encourage the newly revived people and leaders to continue rebuilding, for they had

become discouraged after a month of reconstruction.

3. The *third message* (2:11-19) assured the people of the return of God's favor in their agricultural efforts since they had become obedient in rebuilding the temple.

4. The *fourth message* (2:20-22) was intended to encourage the leader of the rebuilding program, Zerubbabel. He was instructed that God would put down all nations and kingdoms, inferring the liberation of the Jewish nation from foreign domination. Zerubbabel was a "type" of Jesus Christ who would reign someday.

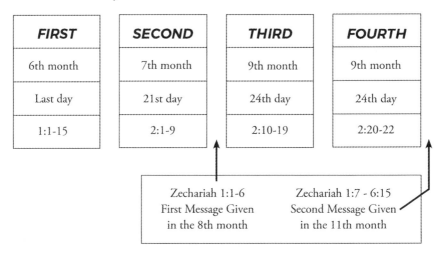

Christians today can find many practical lessons from these four sermons. Christians are involved in building the body of Christ, the church. How are we getting along? Is it a top priority in our lives? Have we grown discouraged in the process so that we want to give up? If Christ loved the church and gave Himself for her, we ought to give ourselves in sacrifice to see the church grow and develop in the earth.

ZECHARIAH (SIXTH CENTURY BC)

Praise God for young people—Christian young people! They can make an impact for God in this world today, and many are doing so. Some of the Old Testament prophets were very young when they began their ministry (Jeremiah and Daniel, for instance). Zechariah 2:4 reveals that Zechariah was just a youth when he received a magnificent vision from God (1:7–6:15). If God wants to (and He often does), He can use young people to do great things for Him. A young Christian should make himself or herself available to God for service. We may never be used to the extent of the great heroes of the Bible, but it is awesome and wonderful to think that God can use us to accomplish some of His work, no matter what our age or our spiritual gifts! God uses men and women who are usable. Pray that He will make you a usable servant!

The Prophet's Name—Zechariah

The name Zechariah belonged to some twenty-eight different men in the Old Testament. It means *Jehovah remembers*. That has great significance for Zechariah's prophecy, for in it he reveals many times that the Lord has not forgotten His people. Neither has He forgotten the many unconditional promises He made to His people centuries earlier through Moses and the prophets. Zechariah was inspired with the hope of the fulfillment of God's great plan for His people Israel, in spite of the fact that their present situation was domination by the Persian Empire. God has His own timetable for accomplishing His plan. Let us not forget that Jehovah remembers!

The Theme of the Book

The theme of Zechariah is twofold: (1) practical messages concerning certain aspects of godly living (1:1–6; 7–8) and (2) predictive messages to inspire faith and hope (1:7–6:15; 9–10). The practical messages concerning godly living addressed certain questions which needed to be answered. The predictive messages addressed the humbled Jewish nation which was struggling for survival and in need of hope to rekindle their spirits and encourage their faith. Zechariah beautifully meets the needs of the nation by his prophetic ministry. And his messages delivered in Jerusalem come down to us as great words of challenge and powerful words of inspiration and hope.

References to the Messiah

Among the many kingdom prophecies there are several references to the Messiah. Zechariah resembles Isaiah and the Psalms in this way.

1. Christ's entry into Jerusalem (9:9; Matt. 21:5)

2. Christ's betrayal by Judas for 30 pieces of silver (11:12-13; Matt. 27:9)
3. Christ being forsaken by His disciples (1:7b; Matt. 26:31b)
4. Christ's death (13:7a; Matt. 26:31a)
5. Christ's second coming to earth (14:3-4; Acts 1:11)
6. Christ being recognized as Messiah when He comes again (12:10; Rev. 1:7)
7. Christ's reign as Priest and King when He returns (14:9; Rev. 11:15ff; 19:11)

Summary of the Book

First Message 1:1-6	Second Message 1:7-6:15	Third Message 7-8	Fourth Message 9-14
8th month, 2nd year of Darius I (520 BC)	11th month, 2nd year of Darius I (520 BC)	9th month, 4th year of Darius I (518 BC)	No date given for this message.

1. A Practical Message Calling for Repentance (1:1-6)

Zechariah challenged the returned exiles to repent, warning them not to repeat the mistakes of their fathers, who did not listen to the prophets (2 Chron. 36:15-16). Rather, they mocked them. Thus, their fathers had reaped God's judgment (2 Chron. 36:17-21). It is often said that we never learn from history. In a sense, Zechariah is making a plea to Israel to let history teach them! Why should the children make the same mistakes as those of the fathers and suffer the consequences? Let us pray that we shall be preserved from ignoring the lessons of the past.

2. A Predictive Message to Inspire Faith and Hope (1:7–6:15)

Zechariah received this message three months after he preached his sermon calling for repentance. Observe several things about it:

- It was received through a vision Zechariah had during the night.
- There are eight distinct parts to the vision; however, the parts are related.

- The vision covers a very great span of time, beginning with the period in which Zechariah lived down to the establishing of the kingdom of Christ on earth for a thousand years.
- In the vision, Zechariah is accompanied by an interesting angel who tells him the meaning of many parts of what he sees.
- The vision is concluded by the crowning of Joshua, the high priest (6:9-15). This crowning is symbolic of our Lord's reign as Priest and King on the earth.
- The vision was meant to inspire faith in the returned exiles for the day in which they lived, and to inspire hope for the future glory of the nation—a nation then subject to the Persian Empire.

Though the promises in the vision are for Israel, not the church, there are abiding principles which may be gleaned which the Christian can apply to his life. As you study through the Old Testament prophets, be sure

Be sure to distinguish between promises and principles.

to distinguish between *promises* and *principles*. Nothing in the Prophets can be construed as a promise to the church. The church and Israel are two different groups, but there are many abiding principles for living which are good for any era.

3. A Practical Message Calling for Reality and Genuineness in the Spiritual Life (7–8)

This third message is dated in the 4th year, 9th month, and 4th day of Darius I (518 BC). The work on the temple had been resumed now for two years. It was probably more than half done.

The Jewish people were concerned about a religious activity they had been practicing for many years since the Babylonian exile began. It was the practice of fasting. Now that the exile was over, they wondered if they should continue to observe fast days. Zechariah did not say yes or no. Why? He discerned that they had a deeper problem than the question about fasting. The deeper problem was dedication to the Lord. The question was all right, but the attitude behind it was carnal. Their attitude demonstrated a lack of heart devotion to Jehovah. Christians sometimes have the same kind of attitude. The attitude of the believer should be, "Lord, what will You have me do?" Let us not call Jesus our Lord and then pursue our own will.

4. A Predictive Message to Inspire Faith and Hope (9–14)

This section is divided into two prophetic messages (chapters 9–11 and 12–14). In it, there are some prophecies which were fulfilled in the period between the Old and New Testaments (404 BC–4 BC). Some were fulfilled in the time of our Lord while He was on earth, and some are yet to be fulfilled in the tribulation period and kingdom age. The two messages are called burdens (9:1; 12:1). A burden is a prediction which is threatening in nature.

The first burden (chapters 9–11) has primarily to do with predictions already fulfilled in the first coming of Christ. Christ is seen as the great world conqueror (chapter 9), the hope of His people (chapter 10), and the rejected Shepherd (chapter 11).

The second burden (chapter 12–14) has primarily to do with predictions yet to be fulfilled. Judah and Jerusalem will be invaded in the last days by the Antichrist (12:1-9), Israel will be converted (12:10–13:9), the second coming of Christ to earth will be accomplished (14:1-7), and the kingdom of Christ will be established on earth. Great days are ahead for Israel. Right now "a partial hardening has come upon Israel, until the fullness of the Gentiles has come in [until the church age has run its course]. And in this way all Israel will be saved" (Rom. 11:25-26).

What a glorious day is ahead! The believer in Jesus Christ will be involved in that day, for the church will return to earth with Jesus Christ when He comes to subdue the earth and establish His one thousand-year reign. But let us not get God's order of events confused. Observe the following time chart:

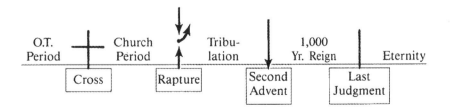

MALACHI (FIFTH CENTURY BC)

Do you doubt that God really loves you? So you couldn't care less about how you worship God! So you think God's laws concerning marriage are out of date! So you feel that the justice of God is a big joke! So you say, "I'm not going to give any of my resources to the Lord!" So you believe that it doesn't pay to serve the Lord! If this is the way you think and feel, then you have a lot in common with the people of Malachi's day. For all these things, so common today, were true of the people of that time.

Doubting God's love for us is probably the most serious of all these, for it sets the stage for a multitude of other sins. If we believe that God doesn't love us, then why should we care about worshiping, obeying, being loyal in our marriage, acknowledging God's attribute of justice, giving him a portion of our resources, and committing our lives to His service? But God does love us, and when we believe this and realize the implications of it in our lives, then we must love Him in return. Our love for Him will be manifest in obedience to His word. Jesus said, "Whoever has my commandments and keeps them, he it is who loves me" (John 14:21).

The nation of Israel in Malachi's day was unevenly divided into two groups: (1) the great majority of the nation doubted God's love and were living in outrageous sin, and (2) a remnant believed God's love (3:16-18) and was characterized by reverence and obedience. What category are you in?

The Prophet's Name—Malachi

Malachi's name means *My messenger.* What a wonderful name that is. It should remind us that we too have a message to take to the nations, for we are all to be ambassadors for Christ. Malachi delivered to God's people a message which was filled with rebuke. But it was given with the intent of turning them back to God so that they might trust in His love. That is a worthy goal for all God's messengers. As a communicator of God's Word, personally or publicly, what is your goal?

The Prophet's Personal History

There is nothing in the book of Malachi or the historical books of Ezra and Nehemiah which relate his personal history. As in the case of some of the other prophets, it has pleased the Holy Spirit to be silent in this case.

The Time of the Prophet's Ministry

The exact time of Malachi's ministry is not given. We know he prophesied in Jerusalem after the exile because he mentions a governor ruling, a condition that did not exist before the exile (Mal. 1:8). We know he prophesied after Haggai and Zechariah who were post-exilic prophets because the temple had been built and was being fully used (Mal. 1:6-14). Finally, certain details found in the book link him to the time of Nehemiah (445–420 BC). What are these details? All of the sins which Malachi rebukes in his prophecy are ones which Nehemiah rebuked in the thirteenth chapter of his book. In other words, there is a very strong parallel between Nehemiah 13 and the book of Malachi. The parallel is so strong that scholars feel it is the same historical situation. Thus, if Nehemiah 13 is dated around 420 BC, then Malachi has the same date. This would make Malachi the last prophet of the Old Testament.

The Theme of Malachi

The theme is God's rebuke of Israel's outrageous sins. This theme is developed in six charges against the nation as seen in the summary.

Summary of the Book

1. Israel has Doubted God's Love (1:1-5)
2. Israel has Despised God's Name (1:6–2:9)
3. Israel has Defiled God's Law (2:10–16)
4. Israel has Disdained God's Justice (2:17–3:6)
5. Israel has Discarded God's Tithes (3:7–12)
6. Israel has Discredited God's Service (3:13–4:6)

Although he gives some future predictions, Malachi is mainly concerned with ministry designed to rebuke and warn. The reader will observe a recurring method of communication by Malachi as he develops his theme: (1) Charges or accusations are made against Israel; (2) These are followed by objections on the part of the accused (in question form); (3) The objections are then answered clearly and no opportunity to respond is given. This is an excellent and effective teaching form. Let us illustrate this from Malachi 1:6-7.

1. The Charge— "O priests, who despise my name …"
2. Objection— "But you say, 'How have we despised your name?'"
3. Answer— "By offering polluted food upon my altar."

We are not told if Malachi's ministry was successful in his day. There is no indication in his prophecy that the people responded in a positive manner. Results are never the responsibility of the prophet. His duty was to speak God's Word clearly and forcefully, hoping that God's people would take heed. That is true for modern communicators of the Gospel. We, like Paul and Apollos, plant and water God's Word, but only God can give the blessing of growth and fruit (1 Cor. 3:5-9). Do your part! God will do His!

LESSON 12 EXAM

Use the exam sheet that has been provided to complete your exam.

1. **The background history for Haggai is found in**
   A. 2 Kings.
   B. Ezra.
   C. Nehemiah.
   D. Esther.

2. **Haggai's name means**
   A. "fortunate."
   B. "favored."
   C. "faithful."
   D. "festal."

3. **The theme of Haggai is**
   A. the rebuilding of the temple in Jerusalem.
   B. the rebuilding of the walls of Jerusalem.
   C. the return to the rule of kings.
   D. the revival of ancient biblical customs.

4. **Haggai's book consists of four messages which were geared to**
   A. stir up and activate.
   B. warn and threaten.
   C. predict the future.
   D. call the people from idolatry.

5. **The name "Zechariah" is a popular one in the Old Testament. It means**
   A. "Jehovah rewards."
   B. "Jehovah remembers."
   C. "Jehovah releases."
   D. "Jehovah reconciles."

6. **The predictive messages in Zechariah were occasioned by**
   A. the people's interest in predictive prophecy.
   B. the downtrodden state of the Jewish nation.
   C. questions brought to Zechariah concerning godly living.
   D. the daily reading of the Law during religious services.

7. **Like Isaiah and the Psalms, Zechariah has several references to**
   A. the Babylonian captivity.
   B. the restoration of the city of Jerusalem.
   C. the Messiah.
   D. the Antichrist.

8. **The name "Malachi" means**
   A. "approved of the Lord."
   B. "guided by God."
   C. "my messenger."
   D. "God's appearing."

9. **We know that Malachi prophesied in post-exile times because**
   A. his prophecy states it clearly.
   B. he is mentioned as a contemporary of Haggai.
   C. he mentions the rule of a governor over Judah.
   D. the New Testament reveals that he did.

10. **Malachi's ministry was mainly concerned with messages designed to**
    A. rebuke and warn.
    B. comfort and console.
    C. teach and inform.
    D. predict the future.

What Do You Say?

What message for your life do you discern in Malachi 3:16-17?

He is the one appointed by God to be judge of the living and the dead. To him all the prophets bear witness that everyone who believes in him receives forgiveness of sins through his name.

—Acts 10:42-43